Of Course You're Angry

Of Course You're Angry

**A Guide
to Dealing
with the
Emotions of
Substance Abuse**

SECOND EDITION

BY
Gayle Rosellini & Mark Worden

 HAZELDEN®

Hazelden
Center City, Minnesota 55012-0176

1-800-328-0094 (Toll Free U.S., Canada, and the Virgin Islands)
1-612-257-1331 (24-hour Fax)
http://www.Hazelden.org (World Wide Web site on Internet)

Library of Congress Cataloging-in-Publication Data
Rosellini, Gayle.
    Of course you're angry : a guide to dealing with the emotions of
substance abuse / by Gayle Rosellini & Mark Worden. — rev. ed.
        p.   cm.
    Includes index.
    ISBN 1-56838-141-7
    1. Alcoholics — Family relationships.   2. Anger.   3. Alcoholics —
Psychology.   I. Worden, Mark.   II. Title.
HV5132.R674 1997
    362.292'3 — dc21   96-37533
                                                                                      CIP
02 01 00 99 98 97   6 5 4 3 2

Book design by Will H. Powers
Cover design by David Spohn
Typesetting by Stanton Publication Services, Inc.

Editor's note
Hazelden offers a variety of information on chemical dependency and related
areas. Our publications do not necessarily represent Hazelden's programs,
nor do they officially speak for any Twelve Step organization.

All the stories in this book are based on actual experiences. All identifying
information has been changed to protect the privacy of the people involved.

*Dedicated
to the memory of
Michelle Abdill
and Roxanne Ellis*

Contents

1. Anger and Recovery 1

2. In the Beginning, the Family Created Anger 13

3. Anger Styles I: To Feel or Not to Feel 23

4. Anger Styles II: Beyond Bad Temper 31

5. Anger Styles III: Nice People 48

6. Resentments 59

7. Conquering Our Common Conceits 72

8. The Ventilation Trap 85

9. Wrangling without Rancor 98

10. Beyond the Serenity Prayer 113

Index 125

About the Authors 131

1

Anger and Recovery

It's after midnight and Donna is furious.

Why do I put up with it? Does anyone really need this torture? Why isn't Jim home yet? He left for his AA meeting at a quarter to eight. It's a quarter to one and he's still gone! The damn meeting only lasts an hour and a half. Where is he? If he's in a tavern—

No, don't even think it. It's been a year. Jim's been sober a year. He wouldn't. He couldn't.

Where is he?

Crouched into a corner of the sofa, Donna huddles in an agony of fear, worry, and resentment.

Questions swirl through her mind. Wasn't Jim's getting sober supposed to make everything better? Wasn't it supposed to be the start of a bright new life, a life unmarred by the turmoil and arguments of the old drinking days? Hadn't she gone to all those meetings and read all those books just like the counselor recommended? Hadn't she accepted the fact that substance abuse is a family disease; that, in her own way, she'd been just as sick as Jim? Hadn't she done her share, for God's sake, to patch together the shreds of a marriage slashed to pieces by too much drinking and too much gambling at the local casino?

She herself hadn't been to the casino in a year. She'd given up bingo and video poker. That hadn't been easy. And when she went to one of her Twelve Step meetings, she came straight home afterwards. Why couldn't Jim do the same?

Where is he?

If recovery was so wonderful, why was their marriage still awful? Why the pounding heart? the clenched jaws? the aching, crushing pressure in her chest every time Jim pulled another one of these stunts? Didn't he know what they did to her?

No, he doesn't care what it does to me. He's too insensitive, too self-centered to care about my feelings. He'd never understand the depth of my fury. He just doesn't care.

Donna groans audibly. She feels like she's going crazy. *What's wrong with me? Why do I feel so much hatred? Why do I feel so much?*

Baffled, she looks down at her mug and sees the dregs of her coffee. *Cold and bitter,* she thinks. *Very appropriate.* Then she tries to shake off her venomous thoughts. *Jim's sober. That's the important thing to remember. I have to concentrate on that. Sobriety comes first. That's what the counselors always say. Sobriety is the most important thing.*

But her anger remains: *Yeah, Jim's sober. Big deal. Nothing else has changed. He's out doing his thing while I sit home, sick with worry.*

The memory of all those terrible nights stabs at her heart. *Why don't I just get a divorce and be done with it? Jim doesn't care. Oh, he pretends to, but all he really cares about is himself. Otherwise, he wouldn't treat me this way, would he? Would he?*

She wants to cry. How many times has she tried to solve these problems? *But what can I do about it? I certainly can't let Jim know how I feel because if I do, if I lose control of my temper for one minute, everything will come pouring out in a roaring flood of anger, a torrent of pain, a relentless surge of savage and ugly resentment.*

And then it will be too late.

She's afraid. If she starts to cry, she might not be able to stop, and it'll all come out, all of it. Their marriage will be shattered by the pent-up fury of her soul. She might start screaming and never be able to stop. And then Jim might drink again.

Headlights flash in the window. Jim is home.

She greets him at the door, her bravely smiling face hiding her anger, masking the inner turmoil. "Hi, honey," she says with a strained voice. The smile on her trembling lips hardens. "You're late."

"You didn't have to wait up," he says defensively. "Some of the guys and I went to the coffee shop after the meeting. Guess I lost track of the time."

"Oh, well . . ." She shrugs. A pretense of indifference. Jim bends to kiss her. Clamping her lips tight, she turns a cheek to his lips, sniffs, inhales deeply. Cigarettes and coffee and stale Old Spice. Safe, friendly smells. *No alcohol.* Donna sighs with relief.

Jim stiffens. "For crying out loud," he complains, a sour smile twisting his mouth. "What did you expect?"

She turns away. "I'm going to bed," she says. "I'm tired."

"Wait." He grabs her arm. "I want to talk."

Shaking loose, she snarls, "If you want to talk, go back to your friends at Denny's." Her voice is low, sarcastic.

Jim's eyes narrow. Sighing, he says, "You wanted me to quit drinking and I did. Now, you're mad because I go to meetings. I can't win."

"I'm not mad." Her voice is flat, her jaw tight. "I'm just tired."

"Yeah, tired. You're always tired." They glare at each other for a moment. Then Jim turns and heads for the bedroom. As he walks away, he mumbles just loud enough for Donna to hear: "One of these nights I may not come home at all." He slams the bedroom door behind him.

Donna stands staring into space, an empty feeling in her

stomach. *We're getting better,* she commends herself. A tear rolls down her cheek. *Neither one of us lost our temper. Maybe things will work out after all.*

Normal Feelings

If you understand what Donna and Jim are feeling, it means one thing: *You're normal.*

Everyone gets angry, feels the arousal of resentment, the turmoil of rage, the heart-thumping seething of fury. We feel irked, exasperated, irritated, vexed, annoyed, enraged.

We may not like to admit it, but all of us experience anger.

Anger is a normal human emotion. To never feel anger is to never be fully human. Yet intense, uncontrolled anger can hurt and destroy, wreaking havoc and pain. Anger—angry people— can kill.

How many spouses have been beaten, children battered and abused, and other loved ones hurt in a storm of savage anger? A cruel blow, once delivered, can never be taken back. All the tearful apologies and gifts given as peace offerings can't erase the pain of physical and verbal punches delivered in anger. Uncontrolled anger can leave ugly scars.

So, what to do? Swallow our anger? Put on a brave, smiling face like Donna? Many of us believe, just like Donna and Jim, that keeping our real feelings hidden gives us greater control of our lives.

The Denial Trap

In fact, almost everyone born before the 1970s was routinely taught to deny their emotional lives. It was a cultural norm. Some of us took that cultural lesson to heart. We became A+ students in not knowing our emotions from our elbows.

But remember: Anger is a normal part of life.

Unfortunately, most of us never had anyone show us how to make anger work for us in a positive and an effective way.

Or in a way that *helps* us and those around us, rather than making our problems worse.

Nope. We were taught to stuff it.

When pushed down and hidden, anger can work like a slow-acting acid splashed on our self-esteem. It gnaws, burns, and corrodes our feelings, leaving nothing but a raw-edged hole, an empty pit of despair. Sometimes, death looks like the only way out. Fantasies of homicide or suicide often keep company with stuffed anger.

So, my recovering friend, what does any of this have to do with *you?*

You haven't murdered anyone and you haven't committed suicide. Sure, you get a little ticked off once in a while. Piqued, perhaps. But ever since you learned about recovery and Twelve Step programs—or your spouse, child, or parent stopped using—life has been a lot better. Really! Honest! It's just that, well, sometimes things just don't go right. And when things don't go right, it's not always so very easy to stay *serene.*

Anger and Recovery

This is a book about *anger,* specifically about anger and the process of recovery from chemical dependency and other forms of addictive living. And that's what all of this has to do with you. With us. Because we're not going to find anyone in this world who's angrier than an addict, with or without our favorite substance of abuse. Unless, of course, we take into account the spouse and kids of the addict.

Addiction spreads far and wide. It's not just alcohol and other drugs. It's also food, gambling, sex, emotions, and relationships. We're not talking about bad habits here; we're talking about *loss of control.*

Coping with addiction—whether it's our own loss of control or someone else's—is hard work. Why? Because addiction doesn't make sense. It undermines our higher values, the things we believe in most, even our faith in the world.

Addiction makes good people behave badly. It makes generous people act selfishly. It makes us hurt the people we love most. And, because we're human, it's perfectly normal for us to experience intense anger as we struggle with addiction.

A startling truth: *Getting into recovery doesn't make all that anger magically disappear.*

Sometimes recovery makes anger worse, for the family anyway. Take addiction to alcohol, for example. At least when the alcoholic is drinking, we have something to blame the anger on. The bottle. The booze. The drunkenness.

We can hate the alcohol, detest the alcoholism, and somehow still manage to love the alcoholic.

Take away the drinking and what do we have left? All that anger with nothing to blame it on! And that doesn't feel good.

We end up confused.

Weren't all the awful family problems supposed to stop once Dad got sober?

Well, he's sober now, but the house is still filled with tension. He doesn't kick in the door and break the dishes anymore. He doesn't launch into drunken tirades like he used to. He doesn't stay out all night and leave us wakeful and terrified that the phone might ring, with a gentle, official word of regret, informing us that Dad was killed in a car crash at 2 A.M.

So, it *is* better. There's a small sense of trust developing slowly, almost as if we're cordial strangers. But there's tension in the air, mixed with all the memories of yesterday's pain.

You see, when addicts take the plunge into recovery, there isn't much change in the family dynamics. The situation—and the anger—in the family is still far from normal, far from healthy.

We're supposed to be happy now, but the pain and anger don't magically disappear. We still have much work to do. And here's why.

Getting clean and sober, by itself, is no guarantee of happiness.

For the addict, it's the starting point, the single-most important thing necessary to begin the process of recovery.

The process.

Remember that. *Recovery is a process, not a destination.*

Sometimes dramatic changes happen in a blinding flash of insight, a sudden and surprising awakening in our minds. Most of the time, however, recovery is a slow and painstaking thing, a snail's crawl to growth, maturity, and happiness.

And the process takes work.

Learning to deal effectively with anger is part of the process, not only for the addicted person, but also for the spouse and children—even adult children—of the addict. Each of us must go through our own recovery process, because addictive behavior doesn't hurt just the addict. It hurts the family, too.

This book isn't just for those of us struggling with our own addictions. It's for the man or woman who loves, or at one time loved, a chemically dependent person. It's for the son or daughter of an alcoholic, the mother or father of a drug addict, the brother or sister of a compulsive eater, and the long-suffering friend of anyone who's gone out of control.

As members of an addictive family, we have special problems with anger.

Why? Because we've been through the wringer. We've suffered.

In addictive families anger is often expressed in extreme ways—through violence, emotional abuse, neglect, or abandonment.

We become afraid of anger. When we express it, we may be overwhelmed by feelings of guilt. Fear, anger, guilt—for us, these emotions are all tied together in a negative way.

Because we're afraid of anger, we tell ourselves something

like, "Well, the drinking has stopped, so let's put all the bad things away and forget they ever happened."

We try to ignore our angry feelings, hoping all the time they'll go away. But they don't. They usually get worse. Then we feel guilty because we're thinking such venomous thoughts and feeling so vicious. And when that happens, we end up behaving in ways that can hurt us and the people we care about.

We have special problems with fear, anger, and guilt.

Our goal is to learn to accept angry feelings as normal. We want to learn to deal with anger without fear and guilt. Most important, we don't want our anger to hurt us or other people.

An important note: The first step in the recovery process is getting straight and sober.

The No. 1 Rule for alcoholics and other addicts:

Sobriety first, then emotional fine-tuning.

Recovery for those of us who love or live with an addicted person does not depend on the other person's recovery. It helps— no doubt about it—if the other person straightens up. But we can begin our own recovery even if that other person continues to spin out of control.

Learning to deal with our anger and resentments, learning to forgive people who have hurt us, and learning to forgive ourselves for the wrongs we have committed can be the most important elements of our own recovery.

Remember: Anger is a normal emotion. Normal emotions don't have to be eliminated. Whether we admit it or not, we all feel angry sometimes. Recovering people are no exception. We will experience anger.

But if we've spent years dulling our emotions by over-using alcohol, other drugs, sex, food, exercise, work, gambling, or you name it . . . well, recovery has the potential to scare the living daylights out of us.

Like Donna, we may fear the intensity of our emotions. She's kept the peace for so long, she truly believes her anger is big enough to destroy herself and her family. Besides that, she secretly has little faith in her husband's strength or his commitment to recovery. She's afraid to talk about her real feelings. She thinks that disclosing her feelings would push him into another drinking binge, or even an affair with another woman. She doesn't want to hurt him or lose him, so she keeps her mouth shut and hopes for the best.

Though Jim is sober and both he and Donna have participated in counseling, they still have big problems in their marriage. Communication problems. Anger problems. They don't yell and scream and kick at each other, but the anger is there in the clenched jaws, the rejected kiss, the cold stares, the slammed doors, the subtle threats.

Unresolved anger, whether openly discussed or not, undermines the recovery process.

Some anger explodes in a white-hot fury. We recognize that kind of anger. We can see it, hear it, and feel it. But there's another kind of anger: controlled, quiet, polite, ice-cold. It often lives in families where an addict has "gone on the wagon," but neither the addict nor the family is working on the *recovery process.*

Deciding to Deal with Anger

For healthy recovery to take place, this anger needs to be acknowledged, dealt with, and resolved. We need to know that there are healthy ways to express anger, that the management of anger can make recovery less stressful and reduce the chance of relapse.

We must be willing to look closely at sensitive areas of our lives, to learn and to risk and to be open to change. We must be willing to work.

We also must realize that we have a natural aversion to dealing with these problems. Why? Because it is painful! But, then, addicted living always causes pain. Yet the pain of recovery is nothing compared with the pain of addiction.

Of course, before you decide to take the risks and do the work needed, you have to want the things that learning to deal with anger can help you discover. Do you, by any chance, want

- To love, and be loved by, your family?
- To like yourself?
- To reduce your anxiety?
- To enjoy sex?
- To become healthier, physically and mentally?
- To enjoy work more?
- To have caring friendships?
- To be less depressed?
- To learn to forgive yourself and others?

Okay, if you want these things, then this book might be exactly what you need. But before you invest your time and energy, there's one more test that might help you. Because this book is for people who want to learn to deal better with anger, you need to be sure you have a problem with anger. Answer true or false to the following statements.

True False

____ ____ 1. I don't show my anger about everything that makes me mad, but when I do—look out!

____ ____ 2. I still get angry when I think about the bad things people did to me in the past.

____ ____ 3. Waiting in line or waiting for other people really annoys me.

____ ____ 4. I fly off the handle easily.

True False

<table>
<tr><td>____ ____</td><td>5.</td><td>I often find myself having heated arguments with the people who are closest to me.</td></tr>
<tr><td>____ ____</td><td>6.</td><td>I sometimes lie awake at night and think about the things that upset me during the day.</td></tr>
<tr><td>____ ____</td><td>7.</td><td>When someone says or does something that upsets me, I don't usually say anything at the time, but later I spend a lot of time thinking up cutting replies I could and should have made.</td></tr>
<tr><td>____ ____</td><td>8.</td><td>I find it very hard to forgive someone who has done me wrong.</td></tr>
<tr><td>____ ____</td><td>9.</td><td>I get angry with myself when I lose control of my emotions.</td></tr>
<tr><td>____ ____</td><td>10.</td><td>People really irritate me when they don't behave the way they should, or when they act like they don't have the good sense God gave lettuce.</td></tr>
<tr><td>____ ____</td><td>11.</td><td>If I get really upset about something, I have a tendency to feel sick later, either with a weak spell, headache, upset stomach, or diarrhea.</td></tr>
<tr><td>____ ____</td><td>12.</td><td>People I've trusted have often let me down, leaving me feeling angry or betrayed.</td></tr>
<tr><td>____ ____</td><td>13.</td><td>When things don't go my way, I get depressed.</td></tr>
<tr><td>____ ____</td><td>14.</td><td>I find it hard to put frustrations out of my mind.</td></tr>
<tr><td>____ ____</td><td>15.</td><td>I've been so angry at times I couldn't remember things I said or did.</td></tr>
<tr><td>____ ____</td><td>16.</td><td>After arguing with someone, I hate myself.</td></tr>
<tr><td>____ ____</td><td>17.</td><td>I've had trouble on the job because of my temper.</td></tr>
<tr><td>____ ____</td><td>18.</td><td>When riled up, I often blurt out things I later regret saying.</td></tr>
<tr><td>____ ____</td><td>19.</td><td>Some people are afraid of my bad temper.</td></tr>
<tr><td>____ ____</td><td>20.</td><td>When I get angry, frustrated, or hurt, I comfort myself by eating or using alcohol or other drugs.</td></tr>
</table>

___ ___ 21. When someone hurts or frustrates me, I want to get even.

___ ___ 22. I've gotten so uncontrollably angry at times that I've become physically violent, hitting other people or breaking things.

___ ___ 23. At times, I've felt angry enough to kill.

___ ___ 24. Sometimes I feel so hurt and alone I feel like committing suicide.

___ ___ 25. I'm a really angry person, and I know I need help learning to control my temper and angry feelings because it's already caused me a lot of problems.

If you answered true to even one of the last four questions, your anger has reached a dangerous level. By answering those difficult questions honestly, you've proven that you have a great deal of emotional courage. That means you're ready to benefit from professional counseling. Don't delay. Find a therapist and take this book with you.

If you answered true to at least five of the other questions, you are about average in your angry feelings, but learning some anger management techniques could make you a happier person.

If you answered true to ten or more of the other questions, you are seriously prone to anger problems. It's time for some serious change.

Perhaps we can help you get your anger under control before it takes your life out of control.

Shall we begin?

2

In the Beginning, the Family Created Anger

For most of us, the crux of our anger recovery plan—our plan to acknowledge, accept, and cope with our angry and aggressive feelings—is that old standby, *knowledge.*

Insight, motivation, and behavior change spring from knowledge.

But let's face it: No matter how much knowledge we have, we will never attain total serenity. Why not? *Because total serenity is not a normal state of being.* Sometimes it's right and proper for us to feel anger, fear, guilt, or sadness.

For example, if someone we love dies or if we're laid off from a job we like or if we cause harm to another person, it's normal for us to experience distress.

Our problem as recovering people is that we tend to blow our negative emotions out of proportion. We get angry or resentful over small incidents. And we stay resentful for a long time. We tend to brood about the wrongs done to us by people and circumstances, even if we don't show our emotions or talk about them.

That's all part of addiction and dependency. We use our substances and behaviors to blot out and control our emotions. We attempt to numb ourselves against reality. And make no mistake here: We're not doing this because we're sissies.

Many of us face a reality filled with pain, problems, and hardship.

Problem Solving and Serenity

Our goal in recovery is to learn how to face these problems with dignity and a reasonable sense of perspective. Amazingly, once we begin doing that, much of our distress lessens. We become better able to cope with our families, jobs, frustrations, and disappointments.

Even though we may never achieve the serenity of a Buddhist monk, we can become happier than we are now. The Serenity Prayer is a valuable guide, teaching us to pray for the serenity to accept what cannot be changed, the courage to change the things we can change, and the wisdom to tell the difference.

But as with most guides, following it is easier said than done. At some point in recovery we must stop paying lip service to change and start to make positive changes in ourselves wherever we possibly can. We must also learn to accept the fact that some things can't be changed. The hard part, as the Serenity Prayer suggests, is learning the difference between the two.

Some Can'ts
- We can't change anybody but ourselves.
- We can't change the past.
- We can't always get our own way.
- We can't always make others do what we want them to do.

Some Cans
- We can change ourselves.
- We can change the present, which then alters our future.
- We can change how we feel when we don't get our way.
- We can change how we act when others don't do what we want them to do.

We can also learn to understand our anger, what sets it off, and how to live with it. It's important for us to know that anger is not some unpredictable and unknowable beast hunkering down inside us, waiting for our defenses to crack, our armor to crumble, our will to weaken so it can lunge out like a roaring monster grabbing control of our mouths and hands and hearts. Anger doesn't have to lead to catastrophe.

Anger is a commonplace human emotion. It is not mysterious, but it is frequently misunderstood. The strain of misunderstood anger can make recovery rockier than it need be. Worse, the uncontrolled expression of anger can lead to bigger problems such as job loss, child abuse, spouse beating, and trouble with the law. It can also lead back to active addiction.

Listen, because this is important: We're not saying that anger—or any other emotion—causes addictive behavior. But we *do* know that the anger we feel and our responses to other people who are angry with us have a lot to do with individual and family recovery.

Here's a bit of knowledge that might help us better understand anger: Much of our anger starts in the family, continues in the family, and stubbornly refuses to go away even if we leave the family.

Anger and the Family

Families are a little like Mount Everest. They make us angry because they're there. It's been said that living in a family generates more anger than people experience in any other social situation.

One of the reasons we feel angrier with loved ones or friends is because we have a pretty good idea of how they will respond to us. We feel safer and more secure in their company. But there are other reasons:

- Close contact provides more opportunities for anger to develop.
- Minor irritations can easily accumulate and fuel deeper anger.
- We are inclined to try to make loved ones change. When they won't, we get angry.
- Loved ones are inclined to try to make us change. When they try, we get angry.

Now, if this is true of normal, happy families, it's quite reasonable to expect that anger problems will be worse in families made dysfunctional by substance abuse and addictive behaviors.

All families coping with substance abuse and addiction possess at least one thing in common—unpredictability.

Depending on the addict's mood or level of substance use, family life can vary from a hilariously happy party atmosphere to one of intolerable brutality—all in the same hour. Anxiety, anger, and fear lurk constantly, even on the best days.

The addictive family, with its unpredictability and ill-defined or nonexistent family roles, may foster helplessness, shame, neglect, insecurity, and mistrust. Such a family creates an atmosphere in which anger flourishes. We should not be surprised to find that many of these feelings remain well into recovery.

What causes the most anger problems in recovering families? It's the past—the things that happened last year, five years ago, fifteen years ago. We recall with burning resentment every injustice, every offense, every wrong committed against us. Never mind that the injury is remembered through a chemical haze. The memory is embedded deep and it festers like an infected wound.

Stockpiling resentments is a skill refined to high art by many substance abusers. But resentment is not their exclusive property. Family members know a thing or two about carrying a grudge. Let's face it: We're all hiding wounds that haven't been allowed to heal—resentment wounds—the lacerations and trauma of bitter anger. Resentment wounds often have an adverse effect on our jobs, marriages, and friendships. And, of course, on our recovery.

Living in an addictive family is painful. Every member of the family experiences uncertainty. Our problem may be as simple as chronic fretting and a feeling of powerlessness. Or we might dread being yelled at and verbally abused. Too often in addictive families physical and sexual abuse keep us terrified for our safety or for the safety of another family member. And we worry our heads off about the addict we love. We make ourselves sick with anxiety, anger, and despair. That's our reality.

The pain is real. The trauma and anger are real. But there's nothing we can do to change the past. All we can change is the way we allow the past to affect us now. And we can't change the people who hurt us either. The only person we have the power to change is ourselves. Luckily, when *we* change, the good effect often rubs off on the people closest to us.

All Members of an Addictive Family Suffer

We've all heard the phrase "addiction is a family disease." The words roll easily off the tongue, and for those of us who have been in treatment for an addiction, the words become a meaningless slogan, almost like a greeting card cliché: "How's it going?" "Have a happy day." "Addiction is a family disease."

Stop and think about it. What do we mean when we say addiction is a family disease?

First, we have to understand that alcoholism and other chemical dependencies are actual physiological disorders that can have severe medical complications. There is abundant scientific evidence that a predisposition toward addiction is inherited. In other words, if we have a close blood relative who is chemically dependent, and if we drink or use other addictive substances, we run a higher than normal risk of developing addiction problems ourselves.

There's more. If we have a close blood relative who is chemically dependent, we also inherit a predisposition to depression. That hits us with a double-whammy because we often use alcohol and other mood-altering drugs in a futile attempt to ease the pain of depression.

If we're angry and depressed, our drugs of choice are most likely to be uppers such as cocaine and methamphetamines, with alcohol to smooth us out. If we're angry and anxious, we'll probably prefer downers such as alcohol, tranquilizers, and marijuana, with an occasional upper to jump-start us when we need to look alive.

We could get real fancy here and talk about the different symptoms and characteristics of each different kind of drug user. But we're not going to do that because, except in an overdose or detox situation, it's not all that important.

What counts is this: If we're messed up on alcohol or other drugs, we've been hurting ourselves and the people who love us for a long time. Regardless of what substance we used or why we used it, we can recover. We can reclaim our lives, and we can live well.

Even though chemical dependency is an actual physiological illness and people don't become addicts on purpose any more than diabetics purposely develop diabetes, family members face old-fashioned taboos about addiction that make us feel ashamed and guilty about living in an addictive family, or even admitting to ourselves that someone we care about has an addiction problem.

We cover up. We pretend the problem doesn't exist or that it really isn't that bad. We put on a good front and try to conduct our day-to-day lives as if every little thing is just fine and dandy, when in reality our lives are chaotic, inconsistent, and filled with anxiety, embarrassment, and dread.

Pretending, covering up, putting on a good front—this pattern of behavior is called *denial* and it's one of the main features of living with addiction. Denial helps us hide our feelings of grief, guilt, and anger. We hide the truth from the outside world, and we hide it from ourselves.

People who love an addict frequently attempt to dull their pain through compulsive behaviors that bring temporary feelings of relief—sex, gambling, shopping, overeating, obsessive dieting or exercise, or Internet addiction, just to name a few examples.

All this substance abuse and compulsive behavior within the addictive family lead to a complex system of multiple problems hidden behind a wall of denial. Family members who manage to avoid addictions and compulsions of their own often find themselves saddled with long-term feelings of depression, shame, or anxiety. Each family member may be suffering alone in his or her own personal hell.

Behind the Wall of Blame and Denial

Blame and denial are simple defense mechanisms that keep us unhappily stuck in that personal hell. These defenses delay the addict and the family members from seeking the help we so desperately need in order to recover.

What happens in the family is this: Nobody talks about IT.

Nobody talks about the disease of addiction, the bad feelings, the unpredictability, the fear. It's as if everyone in the family—the addict, the spouse, the kids—is engaged in a giant conspiracy of silence about the one thing that needs to be brought out into the open: the addiction and all the dysfunctional behaviors that go with it.

Oh, to be sure, there's a lot of talk and blame and

recrimination that skirt the issue, but everyone is so busy protecting and blaming and covering up that real progress is never made.

Unfortunately, this very same process can continue after the addicted family member cleans up, especially if cleaning up happens without the help of a support group or treatment program to guide the way.

The denial—the conspiracy of silence—becomes habitual. It's this conspiracy that affects the non-addicted members of the family so deeply. That's why we call it the family disease.

Everyone—not just the addict—is affected. Spouses, parents, and kids become expert liars. Yes, even the most honest of people learn to look the other way, cover up, overprotect, tell a little fib, and then a bigger fib. Pretty soon, honesty and truth get completely muddled and lost.

The result? Feelings of frustration, low self-esteem, blame, powerlessness, confusion, self-pity, alienation, distrust, and a pervasive sense of aloneness in a hostile world. We learn to hide our real feelings, and we learn distorted and unhealthy ways of expressing them. We know something is terribly wrong with our lives, but we don't quite know how to fix it.

That makes us angry!

And guess what? The majority of addicts suffered from the family disease long before they sampled their first mind-altering substance. They had an addicted parent or grand-parent.

So, is it any wonder that people who live in addicted families have anger problems? The fact that we suffer from angry feelings doesn't make us strange or bad people. We have no reason to be ashamed or guilty about our feelings. After what we've been through, it would be amazing if we *didn't* emerge with more than our share of unresolved conflicts.

Anger is one of the symptoms of the family disease and it lasts long after the addict has cleaned up. Learning to cope with anger is an important part of the recovery process. But we have to remember that not all anger looks alike nor is it always readily recognized.

Anger can take many forms. We readily recognize shouting or fighting as angry actions. We see the red faces, hear the harsh words, and sometimes feel the blows. But anger can take other forms: Depression, manipulation, the silent treatment, compulsive eating, vandalism, and suicide can mask what's really going on under the surface—festering rage.

Reality Check

Let's stop for a moment and check your knowledge and attitudes. Answer these questions with a yes or no.

1. Do you accept anger as a normal and commonplace human emotion?
2. Do you think learning to understand, accept, and cope with your angry feelings is an important part of your personal recovery plan?
3. Are you beginning to accept the idea that living in an addicted family breeds angry feelings?
4. Are you willing to believe you have no reason to feel guilty or ashamed of your feelings?
5. Can you see that angry feelings can continue even after recovery begins, or after you no longer live with an addict?
6. Do you understand that anger can be expressed in many ways, some of which might not look like anger on the surface?

If you can answer yes to these questions, congratulations! You've already gained some knowledge about anger and you're developing healthier attitudes about your feelings.

If you can't honestly say yes to all six questions yet, don't despair. Try this instead: Go back and review what you've read. Think about it. Talk about it with a friend. Talk about it with someone who has also lived in an addictive family. Compare notes.

And remember: We can't become instant anger experts. There's still a lot to learn! Let's start by looking at some different anger styles.

3

Anger Styles I: To Feel or Not to Feel

The Spock Syndrome: Born Vulcan

In the past, when I've worked with addicted people and their families, I asked this question: If you could be like any popular person or fictional character, whom would you choose?

One person regularly received about 80 percent of the votes. My clients, male and female alike, disclosed that if they could be anyone, they'd want to be Mr. Spock.

As you undoubtedly know, Mr. Spock is the half-human, half-Vulcan first officer of the *Starship Enterprise*. On the classic television series *Star Trek* and in subsequent movies, Spock captured the imagination of the world.

When insulted by Dr. McCoy, when frustrated by balky anti-matter devices, when under attack by hordes of nasty Klingons, Spock coolly raises an eyebrow and murmurs, "Fascinating."

Captain Kirk seethes, gyrates, agonizes, and sweats. Spock merely observes the situation, checks his data, applies the proper logical solution, and saves the *Enterprise* for one more voyage. Although Kirk is every bit as heroic as Spock, and certainly more human and humane, never once have I had a client tell me they'd like to be Captain Kirk.

You see, Captain Kirk is so . . . well, *emotional*. He hurts, he suffers, he yells, he even cries. Unlike Spock, Kirk *feels*.

But don't we all?

To my way of thinking, Kirk is a much better emotional role model than Spock, simply because he is so human, he feels so much, and he expresses those feelings without trampling other people. When his base emotions (we *all* have them)—vengeance, hostility, aggression, rage—thunder to the surface, he struggles with them, he acknowledges them, and he rises above them. Of course, the process is painful. Much of life is.

Perhaps that's why so many of my clients admire Spock's emotional style. Spock rises above pain, above anger, above the embarrassingly sloppy emotions we humans are heir to. If we could be like Spock, we would be spared all the pain of being human.

We would be strong and unflappable. We would have the essence of courage—grace under pressure. But, try as we might, none of us will ever be able to duplicate Spock's emotional style. We're not hewn from the red stone of planet Vulcan; we have none of Spock's green blood in our veins. We're stuck with the *human* condition.

How much better it is to admire Kirk with all his emotionality! At times, we all experience intense emotions. We behave erratically. When under pressure, we sweat like horses, our fingers tremble, and our stomachs churn. But, like Kirk, we also have inner reserves of strength, intelligence, and common sense to counterbalance these imperfections in our character.

Interestingly, no one has ever told me they'd want to be like Data, the popular android character on *Star Trek: The Next Generation*. Data is a machine. He has no emotions at all. Spock, who is half-human, experiences deep friendships, caring, and loyalty. The good stuff.

There's nothing wrong with wanting the good stuff . . . as long as we remember that Spock is fiction and we're the real thing.

Different Strokes for Different Folks

Let's look at four different emotional styles, four different ways of expressing anger: "Bulldozer," "Brick," "Soulful One," and "Lightheart." Almost everyone fits into one of these categories, although it's rare to find a person who is "pure to type." It's more common to be mainly of one temperament style, with a tinge of one of the other types to spice up the personality.

Once we understand which style best fits us (and those we care about), we can work to eliminate our weak points while developing our strengths.

THE BULLDOZER

The Bulldozer is always pushing, reaching, succeeding. If a job needs doing, a Bulldozer gets it done. Bulldozers refuse to believe there is anything about them that might need improving, adjusting, or changing, but they can see your weaknesses a mile away. Successful executives, athletes, and entertainers are often Bulldozers. So are many mothers. Their motto in life is, "I'm right and you're wrong." They'd be impossible to tolerate if they weren't so darned successful and charming.

Strengths	Weaknesses
Leader	Bossy
Forceful	Short-tempered
Outspoken	Rude
Decisive	Controlling
Firm	Unsympathetic
Independent	Selfish
Competitive	Aggressive
Productive	Workaholic
Daring	Insensitive
Convincing	Manipulative
Strong-willed	Stubborn

Strong Points

- The Bulldozer is a great worker and can accomplish wonders in a short time.
- The Bulldozer is persistent and is not easily discouraged.
- Bulldozers are not afraid to stand up for what they believe is right.

Problems

- The Bulldozer can be a bully.
- The Bulldozer is insensitive to the needs of others.
- The Bulldozer always has to be right.

Anger Style

Bulldozers can be short-tempered and argumentative. Because they always want to be right, they don't always listen to other people's opinions. They tend to disregard the feelings of others. Bulldozers win arguments, but are often resented and disliked.

Focus of Change

As a Bulldozer, you'll need to learn to listen. Try to accept the idea that other people have a right to be different from you, and just because they are different doesn't mean they are wrong. When talking with another person, practice these statements: "How do you feel about that? What do you think? What's your opinion?"

THE BRICK

While lacking Mr. Spock's heroism, the Brick comes closest to the Vulcan's emotional flatness. Avoiding conflict, extremes, and excesses, the Brick travels down the middle road, offending no one, doing what is expected, and not asking for attention. Because the Brick doesn't like to make decisions, he or she makes a perfect follower. Bricks make pleasant company and great diplomats. Their motto is, "Don't rock the boat."

Strengths	Weaknesses
Agreeable	Compromising
Tactful	Boring
Friendly	Superficial
Obedient	Submissive
Inoffensive	Bland
Attentive	Uninvolved
Patient	Indifferent
Contented	Aimless
Forgiving	Fearful
Obliging	Indecisive

Strong Points

- The Brick is adaptable and can make the best of most any situation.
- The Brick is diplomatic and doesn't like to hurt others' feelings.
- Bricks can have a dry sense of humor.

Problems

- The Brick is wishy-washy.
- The Brick is uncommunicative.
- The Brick is stubbornly boring.

Anger Style

Bricks refuse to talk about their feelings because they fear conflict. Their anger shows up in a chronic lack of enthusiasm for the plans, ideas, and wishes of family and friends. Bricks quietly pour cold water all over another person's excitement but never come out and say, "No, you can't do that." Since a Brick refuses to make a decision or take responsibility, it's always somebody else's fault if something goes wrong.

Focus of Change

If you're a Brick, you'll need to learn to talk about feelings and desires. Try to show enthusiasm when someone you care about is excited over a new project, idea, or plan. When talking with another person, practice these statements: "Hey, that's a neat idea! That's really exciting! Tell me more."

THE SOULFUL ONE

The Soulful One is the mind, heart, and spirit of humanity. Soulful Ones carry the weight of the world on their shoulders. Feeling unique, alienated, and lonely, they find that happiness is always just out of their grasp. Natural helpers, Soulful Ones are often enmeshed in other people's problems. They lean toward the arts and the helping professions—counseling, teaching, nursing, social work, and motherhood. Their motto is, "Woe is you, so let me help." (And woe is me, too!)

Strengths	*Weaknesses*
Decorous	Compulsive
Loyal	Insecure
Thoughtful	Moody
Analytical	Depressed
Self-sacrificing	Resentful
Perfectionistic	Hyper-critical
Benevolent	Unforgiving
Idealistic	Naive
Sensitive	Thin-skinned
Persevering	Vengeful

Strong Points
- The Soulful One is sympathetic to the plight of the needy.
- The Soulful One is a giving, caring person.
- Soulful Ones can be counted on when the chips are down.

Problems
- The Soulful One is frequently depressed and insecure.
- The Soulful One puts unreasonable demands on family and friends, and usually ends up disappointed and hurt.
- The Soulful One wants unconditional approval.

Anger Style

Soulful Ones most often try to make the other person feel guilty and apologetic for letting them down. Because they are so insecure, they are afraid of alienating the love of family and friends, so they don't express their anger directly. They use hurt looks, sighs, and the cold shoulder. They also direct their anger inward, sometimes becoming compulsive eaters or semi-invalids.

Focus of Change

Being a Soulful One, you'll need to learn to lower your expectations of other people. Practice being open and honest about your needs without trying to make other people feel guilty if they can't or won't meet them. When talking with another person, practice these statements: "What I need is . . ." "What I want is . . ." "I feel angry because . . ."

THE LIGHTHEART

All butterflies and rainbows, the Lightheart is the life of the party, a joy—and a frustration. When things get heavy, these people dance away singing and laughing. Their motto is, "Call me irresponsible and party hearty." They often skip from job to job, but there's only one occupation that really suits them: independent wealth.

Strengths	Weaknesses
Optimistic	Unrealistic
Affectionate	Unfaithful
Persuasive	Talkative
Young at heart	Immature
Spontaneous	Forgetful
Sociable	Loud
Enthusiastic	Undisciplined
Dramatic	Grandiose
Convincing	Untrustworthy
Cheerful	Shallow

Strong Points
- Lighthearts are fun, lively, and popular.
- Lighthearts make new friends easily.
- Lighthearts can live by their wits.

Problems
- Lighthearts have difficulty developing deep and lasting relationships.
- Lighthearts are insensitive and their wit can turn cruel.
- Lighthearts lack sympathy for other people's problems.

Anger Style
Lighthearts shrug off anger quickly, and because they lack empathy, they can't understand why everybody makes such a fuss over their antics. When the going gets tough, Lighthearts throw tantrums, make stylish scenes (best performed before a large audience), and disappear until the heat dies down. But Lighthearts are so charming, they're often able to get the people they've hurt to throw them a lavish going-away party. Friends and family will miss the Lightheart, even while they're stuck with cleaning up the mess the Lightheart has left behind.

Focus of Change
If you're a Lightheart, it will help if you learn to accept responsibility. Try not to run from problems and difficult situations. Instead, stick with a problem until you have solved it. When talking with others, practice LISTENING to what *they're* saying instead of to the music of your own voice.

· · · · · · · · ·

Each of these four anger styles can result in an interesting and healthy personality. No single anger style is better than another.

Each anger style can be seen in simply marvelous people. Each anger style can produce horrors! When taken to an extreme, an emotional style can be downright disabling. Read on, and learn about two dangerous ways of expressing anger.

4

Anger Styles II: Beyond Bad Temper

Violence in Everyday Life

Do you know someone like this? They hit first and ask questions later. But they usually go after someone smaller or weaker than they are, someone who can't, or won't, hit back. Walls, dishes, windows, and clothes are punched, thrown, smashed, or ripped. Apologies and gifts sometimes follow a rampage, but almost inevitably more violence follows, too.

We're not talking here about hardened criminals, gangsters, muggers, serial killers, or rapists. Career criminals may wreak havoc in the streets, but let's face it, few of them read self-help books. They don't care who they hurt—but you do.

We're talking about ordinary folks, people who appear respectable, hardworking, even kindly to strangers.

You see, most violent people don't hurt strangers.

Recent national crime statistics show that two-thirds of murder victims are killed by a family member, friend, or acquaintance. When it comes to non-fatal assaults, the chances are even greater that the victim and perpetrator know each other.

We hurt the people closest to us—our mates, children, siblings, parents, and friends.

Paradoxically, many violent people are well liked and

respected by friends and co-workers. They are often considered pillars of the community. Because their everyday behavior looks so unlike the violence simmering under the surface, most people who know them deny the truth, even when it stares them in the face.

Blame the Victim

For example, Maynard was a well-respected family therapist. He was given awards by the Chamber of Commerce and by the Governor's Commission on the Family. He regularly received more than $1,000 to give inspirational speeches around the country on the importance of the family.

After Maynard won a regional award as father of the year, his teenage son spilled the beans. The son stood up in a public meeting and said that his father might be an inspiration to people who didn't know him, but at home he was a tyrant. He beat his wife into cowering submission, threatened his children, and lived a life of total hypocrisy.

Maynard didn't miss a beat. He admitted he had problems with his temper, that he'd treated his wife and children badly at times. But he'd learned from the experience and through prayer and introspection, he'd become a better and wiser person. His own personal tragedies guided him in helping other people.

The audience applauded.

And while applauding, they whispered among themselves about what a difficult woman Maynard's wife was. Moody, you know. Hard to get along with. The consensus seemed to be that poor Maynard had a difficult cross to bear.

So, what was wrong with the people who found fault with Maynard's victims while sympathizing with him? Were they crazy or what?

In all likelihood, they were normal people reacting in a normal way for our culture. Our culture tells us that good people don't respond violently unless they're pushed beyond the limit. Friends don't believe that violence is possible unless . . . well, of course, there's only one explanation: The victim must have done something *really awful* to provoke the attack.

The victim *must have had it coming.*

This twisted logic keeps the violence alive. It's called *blaming the victim.* It lets the abuser off the hook, keeps the victim quiet, and allows the violence to continue.

Let's get this straight: Nobody deserves to be slapped, punched, brutalized, threatened, or terrorized.

Physically hurting or threatening other people is wrong.

So, Maynard's wife was moody. So what? Maybe she was moody because she was scared and ashamed and felt terribly alone. Her moodiness did not excuse Maynard's brutality. Yet, when the family violence was revealed, it was the wife who was criticized. Is it any wonder that victims of domestic violence too often suffer in silence?

Venus and Mars Slug It Out

There's not one iota of evidence that men, as a group, are any angrier than women or vice versa. But it doesn't take a controlled scientific study to tell us that men show their anger and rage more. For proof, all we have to do is look at the violent crime statistics. Males far outnumber females as perpetrators of violence. Most victims of street crime are also males.

But when it comes to domestic violence, the vast majority of victims are women and children. This is true whether we're talking about a slap or a homicide.

Citizens in Oregon were recently shocked when crime statistics showed that of the ten most dangerous cities to live in the state, eight were small towns. What made these rural communities so dangerous? *Domestic violence.* The police can keep crime off the streets in small-town America, but they can't protect women and children in their own homes.

Men are more frequently violent than women, and research indicates that women are more frequently diagnosed with depression. Perhaps men turn their anger outward, while women turn it inward. Women take more psychotropic medication (drugs that act on the mind) than men and are hospitalized more often for depressive illness than men.

However, when it comes to violent behavior, we all know outspoken women who can rival any man in bellowing and belligerence. Similarly, we know soft-spoken men who are nurturing and mild-mannered.

We learn how to express our emotions—all our emotions, not just anger—at an early age. We learn in our families. We watch our parents and our brothers and sisters, and we either imitate them or rebel against them. We are rewarded for certain behaviors and punished for others. And the rewards are often arbitrary and inconsistent. All the time we're feeling and learning.

Although emotions—love, fear, anger, joy—are innate in all of us, how we interpret and express them is learned in our families. We all *feel,* but we don't all *show* those feelings in the same way.

Feeling an emotion and expressing an emotion are two distinct things. Feeling is innate. Expressing is learned. Unfortunately, some of us learn to express our feelings through violence.

Substance Abuse and Violence

Crime statistics show that substance abuse goes hand in hand with violence. That's why violence is common in chemically dependent families, and it's not always the addict who's doing the hitting and breaking. The spouse and children of an addict can be so consumed by frustration and rage that they strike out—a mother abusing her children, a child abusing a pet. Violence is contagious and spreads from the strongest to the weakest member of the family.

Dad hits Mom. Mom hits Sissy. Sissy hits baby brother. Baby brother kills the goldfish.

People who discover they can get away with ranting and raving, intimidating, hitting, kicking, breaking, and hurting have learned an extreme way of expressing emotion.

Even after the addict gets clean and straight, the violence may continue unless we learn to channel aggressive feelings into less dangerous pathways.

People prone to violence seem to snap—become their most violent—under pressure.

Freeing ourselves from substance abuse improves our lives tremendously, but it does not guarantee us a life free of pressure. In fact, many of us will find the first few years of recovery to be more stressful than ever. Before, we were numbing ourselves from the harsh realities of our lives. Now, we're facing life with clear heads. We're solving problems we avoided in the past. That's pressure!

Recovery in Chaos: Don Snaps

Being sober for two years didn't prevent Don from snapping. The owner-operator of an eighteen-wheeler, Don was under a great deal of financial and emotional stress. He drove long-haul, which meant he was out on the road for days at a time in all sorts of weather. He slept little and ate more junk food than his body could handle.

After a trip from Seattle to the East Coast, down to Florida, back over to Los Angeles, and then back up I-5, he came home a week before Christmas to discover that his wife had left him, taking their seven-year-old daughter with her. For Don, it was a crushing blow. He felt confused and frightened, jealous and stunned. His fluctuating emotions jerked him around like a puppet on a string.

In a panic, Don called the counselor who had helped him get sober. At first, Don talked calmly. Then the counselor asked a question Don didn't like and Don went berserk. The counselor recalls it this way:

"Don was upset when he called, but he seemed to be in control. As I asked him questions, his conversation grew progressively fragmented, disjointed.

"Finally, he said, 'I just don't know what to do. Why did— why did she—I can't understand . . .' There was silence on his end of the line and then I heard him moan, 'Oh, God!' It was a pitiful wail, and then he bellowed like a wounded bull."

The counselor shakes his head in disbelief. "I tell you, it made the hair stand up on my arms. It made me shiver. I've never heard anything like it."

The counselor heard the telephone receiver thud to the floor. Then came the crunch of breaking furniture, the crash of breaking glass. And in the background, Don's heavy breathing and groaning rasped loudly. He had been transformed almost instantly into a hurt and enraged beast, inarticulate except for the eerie guttural wailing that came as he wrecked his house. The rampage went on for several minutes. Then silence.

"Don? Don?" The counselor called into the telephone. The heavy, labored breathing came closer to the phone. "I'm . . . I'm sorry," Don said. "Something . . . I guess I just snapped."

Don snapped, all right. And that wasn't the first time it had happened. His rampages were the cause of his wife's departure. "After living for ten years with a Jekyll and Hyde personality," she explained, "I left. When Don got sober, I thought everything would be better, and for a little while it was. But his unpredictable temper finally drove me away. I never knew what was going to happen. He might come in the door all smiles, but if he didn't like what I fixed for dinner, he'd go into a frenzy, calling me names, breaking things, hitting me. I couldn't take it any longer."

She didn't want to be around Don when he snapped. And she wanted to get her daughter out of harm's way.

So why did Don snap? There's probably no single reason. Money worries, pressures from work, too many cigarettes, too much coffee, frayed nerves—they all add up. However, his behavior typifies a common, frightening trait found among people prone to violence: a bizarre lack of proportion. There's no discrimination between a minor irritation and a major catastrophe. A burned dinner evokes a response as intense as the loss of a family member.

Drinking and other drug use lower our inhibitions and make us more likely to act impulsively. Lowered inhibitions can incite family violence. But Don had successfully dealt with a serious drinking problem. He had stopped drinking. As the saying goes, he was dry but not recovered.

If rage reactions continue after we achieve sobriety, we must acknowledge that we are not yet recovered. We need to seek further treatment specifically for our anger problems.

Frying Pan Revenge

Men aren't the only ones who engage in physical violence. Hot lines all over the country are reporting an increase in calls from men who have been beaten by their wives. One woman, infuriated by her husband's drinking and late hours, waited until he fell asleep in their bed, then tied him up in the sheets and beat the living daylights out of him with a cast-iron skillet. He went to the hospital. She went to jail.

Violent women, however, don't usually target their husbands for physical abuse. They hit their children. Most child abusers were themselves abused as children. They learned young that "might makes right." They learned to express their anger and frustration with their fists.

Both men and women abuse children, and older children have been known to hurt younger ones. The cycle goes on and on. Do you see the pattern?

Violent people don't beat up people who are bigger and stronger than they are. Men beat up smaller men, weaker women, and children. Big kids hurt little kids. Women abuse children, and, when furious enough, women get themselves an equalizer—a gun or a cast-iron skillet—and attack the man when he is vulnerable. Even the biggest man crumples when hit with lead.

The Myth of the Uncontrollable Temper

People with violent tempers are often described as *uncontrollable.* "I couldn't help it," they rationalize. "I couldn't stop myself."

Nonsense! Even the most violent people control themselves most of the time.

For example, only a deranged person would run out into the middle of the street, flag down a Hell's Angels motorcycle gang, and yell, "Hey! I'm mad as hell and I want to fight!"

If the violent expression of anger is truly an uncontrollable and unstoppable urge, why, then, do we let the motorcycle gangs drive merrily by while we wait to get home to clobber the wife or kids?

The answer is simple. Even when we seem gripped by the claws of uncontrollable rage, we're still making lightning-quick, *rational* decisions. We're saying to ourselves, "Can I get away with this? How badly will I get hurt if I start hitting? Is it worth the risk? Yes, I think it is." *Pow!*

We choose to be violent.

Yes! Yes, we really do this! We're really thinking these kinds of thoughts, really making a *rational* decision. Unfortunately, these thoughts flash through our heads like meteors on a sunny day. The bright light of our rage and denial blinds us to the process. We don't remember *deciding* to go berserk. We aren't aware that the decision-making process even occurred. But it did!

If we doubt the idea that we actually make rational decisions to be violent, all we have to ask ourselves is this: When was the last time we challenged a motorcycle gang? Or the karate champ of the West Coast? Or the three-hundred-pound gorilla guarding the stage door of our favorite performer? See? When necessary, we can control our uncontrollable tempers. *We pick our fights.*

Now, think about this for a minute: If this rational thinking process is going on in our heads when we're in the throes of intense emotion, if we really *can* control our tempers when it's in our selfish best interest to do so, just think what a powerful tool this rational thinking process can be if we become aware of it, if we use it, if we learn ways to practice control on a daily basis.

When to Seek Help

We can learn to control our violence, but we may need help. How do we know when we need more than self-help? Ask yourself the following questions. In the last twelve months,

1. Have you hit, slapped, choked, kicked, punched, bitten, strapped, burned, pushed, shaken, thrown, or beaten another person when you were angry? The point is, have you hurt another person during an argument? (We're not asking how badly you hurt them—that's often a matter of luck. Today's grazing slap can be tomorrow's knockout punch. Or death blow.)

2. Have you abused a child in any of the above ways? *Look:* We're not talking about a light swat on the bottom to discipline a child who has run out into the road. But if you spank a child hard enough to leave a bruise or welt; if you kick or slap a child; or if you shake a child until his or her head hurts, you have an anger problem—one that can permanently harm your child.

3. When angry, have you on more than one occasion broken dishes or windows, hit walls, torn up clothes, destroyed furniture, thrown objects about, or vandalized your own or someone else's property? Not all violent people attack other people. Breaking every dish in the house may be better than hitting your child, but it's not a rational way to deal with anger.

4. Have you purposely injured or tortured (or even killed) an animal because you were angry? Children and teenagers often take their anger out on cats, puppies, and other small animals. This is a sign of serious emotional disturbance.

5. Have you waved a gun, club, or knife at someone when you were angry? We don't mean a burglar here. Grabbing a weapon when you're angry is extremely dangerous. Even if you don't intend to do anything more than scare the person, there's no guarantee that someone won't get hurt accidentally.

6. Have you been involved in a traffic accident because your anger affected your driving? A car can be a deadly weapon, too often with innocent bystanders as victims.

If you answered yes to even one of these questions, you have a problem with violent behavior. *Remember:* Recognizing a problem is the first step toward solving it.

Many fine people use physical force because they don't know any other way to solve problems. For example, Linda, a modest, soft-spoken Presbyterian who was the head of the PTA and treasurer of the League of Women Voters, slapped her children across the face with an open hand if they disobeyed her or sassed her. That's how she had been disciplined as a child. No one had ever told her it was wrong until she sought family counseling because all her children were failing in school.

Linda went to counseling to talk about her uncontrollable children—she wanted the therapist to know how difficult it was to deal with sassy and disobedient kids.

Linda's therapist immediately keyed on the way Linda disciplined her kids. The therapist's first goal was to help Linda get control of her own anger. It wasn't easy, because Linda didn't feel there was anything wrong with her own behavior.

But gradually, she began to realize how ineffective and harmful her punishment was—how she was harming her children. She stopped slapping them.

Over time, Linda learned other, more effective ways to discipline her kids. She also traced her own hair-trigger temper back to the anger and humiliation she had felt every time her parents slapped her face. And slowly, with counseling, Linda's family began to know happiness.

Linda's experience proves that people prone to violence can change their ways. However—and this is a big however—you may not be able to do it on your own. You're likely to need professional help.

Getting the Right Kind of Help

If you are chemically dependent and not already a member of Alcoholics Anonymous or Narcotics Anonymous, the time to join is right now. AA or NA can do more than simply dry you out. These self-help groups can help you reach full recovery in the very best way. Not by magic or by feel-good pills, but by working a recovery program with other folks who care, one day at a time. They're in the phone book and they're free. You will be welcomed and comforted the moment you walk in the door. So don't delay.

You may also need to become involved in individual or group therapy. But beware. You need therapy that will deal directly with your specific problems of anger and violence. This means you may have to shop around.

Traditional Freudian psychoanalysis, involving several sessions a week over a period of years, is not recommended in your case. Your self-esteem is not the primary issue, nor do you need to explore your past lives to discover the deep karmic reasons for your harsh temper. These may be entertaining and even productive areas to explore later, but first: *You need treatment that will intervene in your violent behavior NOW!* You don't have time to explore your childhood in search of some hypothetical "real" underlying cause of your problems before you change your behavior. *You need to stop the violence now.* As therapy continues, you'll have time to delve deeply into your psyche. But that comes *after* you've addressed the issue of your violent behavior.

What to Look for in a Therapist

Look for these qualities in a therapist:

- Knowledge and experience in treating substance abuse *as a primary disorder,* not as a symptom of some other psychological ailment. (Therapists who do not understand substance abuse can do you more harm than good.)
- An emphasis on cognitive, behavioral, or rational-emotive therapy. This type of structured, short-term therapy focuses on the "here and now" and works to change your attitudes and behavior.
- A therapist who does not recommend the use of tranquilizers. There is no evidence that tranquilizers help extremely angry or violence-prone people. In fact, tranquilizers or sleeping pills may make the situation

worse because these drugs lower inhibitions just like alcohol and street drugs.

Recovery and Antidepressant Medications

Substance abusers must be extremely wary of tranquilizers. For us, tranquilizers and sleeping pills are just another way to get high. Antidepressant medications, such as Prozac or Zoloft (among many others), are a different matter. These medications do not get you high and are not habit-forming. They might help you. However, we urge caution:

- These medications should not be used with alcohol or other drugs that get you high.
- These medications are not a substitute for a treatment program or Twelve Step group.
- You must tell your doctor about your problems with substance abuse. Some antidepressant medications are combined in one pill with a tranquilizer. *Recovering people must avoid tranquilizing medications.* The risks for us far outweigh any benefit such medications might bring.

Always tell your doctor about your problems with substance abuse.

Finding a Therapist

How do you find a therapist? This is sometimes difficult. You could ask your family doctor for a recommendation or you could call your local mental health center. Many hospitals offer psychological services. One of the best ways, however, is to ask your friends. Have they seen a therapist who has been effective in helping them improve their lives?

In seeking out a counselor, don't be shy. You have every right to ask them about their background, training, philosophy, methods, and fees before you sign up for a course of counseling.

And don't be coy. Tell the counselor right up front, "I'm an alcoholic. I have an anger problem. I beat my wife." Or whatever words apply to your particular situation.

It may be embarrassing to admit, but you must tell the truth if you want to change. So here's a chance to be honest about your faults in a safe place, where the object is not to punish, but to help.

And remember: Counselors are not mind readers. You have to tell them what you think your problem is. The counselor may uncover other problems you aren't aware of, but don't waste time playing guessing games. The counselor might not ask the right questions. *It's your job to honestly reveal your problems.*

Don't lie to your counselor.

Do You Need a Psychiatrist?

If we need help for emotional or mental health problems, we may wonder if we need to see a psychiatrist. A psychiatrist is a medical doctor who has taken special post-graduate training in the area of mental illness. Unfortunately, this special training does not always include the study of substance abuse as a primary disorder or as a family illness.

Because psychiatrists are medical doctors, they can prescribe and monitor medications for depression, anxiety, and other emotional problems. Some people with substance abuse problems also have problems with depression and anxiety. They can benefit from carefully monitored medication. Psychologists, social workers, counselors, and other therapists who are not medical doctors cannot prescribe medication.

That can leave us stuck between a rock and a hard place. The rock is the medical doctor who isn't trained to treat substance abuse; the hard place is the substance abuse therapist who can't prescribe medication.

Fortunately, psychiatrists and substance abuse therapists frequently develop working relationships that make it possible for their patients to receive the best care possible. The psychiatrist will often prescribe and monitor medication, seeing the patient only once every few months. In the meantime, the therapist and the patient meet with each other regularly to work on pressing emotional issues.

Some family physicians and internists have become skilled at prescribing medication for emotional problems. Our personal physician may be willing to work with our therapist to ensure that we receive all the help we need.

But we must be cautious. No one has invented a pill or potion that will cure alcoholism, drug addiction, other substance abuse, or the family illness of substance abuse. Medication alone will not be our salvation. Our recovery comes from our willingness to participate in treatment, therapy, or support groups that *directly* address the problem of substance abuse.

So, do you need a psychiatrist? Well, maybe. And then again, maybe not. The answer depends upon the skill and training of the psychiatrist. If you do choose to consult a psychiatrist about your problems, just make sure you choose a psychiatrist who understands substance abuse.

What if you are a child abuser? Some states require counselors to report all confessions of child abuse to the authorities. Please don't let this prevent you from getting help. Your child's well-being, even his or her life, may depend on your having enough courage to face this problem head-on.

If there is a child abuse hot line in your area, call it and ask for help. You won't have to give your name.

Get Help If You're the Victim

What if you are not the person with the violence problem? What if you're the victim of someone else's violence? You need help, too. You probably feel frightened, guilty, and alone. Please, now is the time to reach out for help!

There are several things you can do. First, if there is a battered person's shelter or help group in your area, call them. You *don't* have to move into a shelter to receive advice and counseling from such organizations. They can offer you moral support and guidance, acceptance, and understanding on the telephone or in person.

Guidance and understanding are crucial as you take your first timid steps out of your victim role.

Here's another suggestion that works. The next time you are the victim of violence, call the police and *press charges.* Police records show that if the violent person (usually a husband, stepfather, or boyfriend) in a "family disturbance" is arrested and removed from the home, even for a few hours, the chances of future family violence are dramatically decreased.

It doesn't matter whether offenders are convicted of the assault or disorderly conduct charges. What does matter is that offenders learn that they must pay the consequences if they start hitting. If they know they can't hit you and get away with it, they'll think twice before knocking you around again. So, call the police! Holler for help. Don't allow yourself to be the victim. You don't deserve to be beaten!

And that brings us to another point. Victims of violence often feel guilty, as if they deserve to be abused. Unfortunately, our society often reinforces this view. Many women who suffer from low self-esteem and dependence upon the men who beat them feel they have no choice but to put up with the violence. Don't you believe it!

You have the right to live without fear of violence. Don't let anyone tell you that you must enjoy getting beaten up or else you wouldn't stay. Booshwah! Hogwash!

You may need professional help to increase your self-esteem, increase your independence, and muster the gumption to stand up for your rights. Don't wait for the violent person in your life to make the first move toward recovery. It's up to you. Get help now!

5

Anger Styles III: Nice People

Do you know anyone who is self-sacrificing, considerate, idealistic, and sensitive? Loyal and faithful? Someone you can always count on? Certainly not one of those selfish types always seeking to be the center of attention, always clamoring, "Me, me, me." But someone who's thoughtful, willing to share. Someone you'd like to be around, the perfect mother and wife, the perfect friend. An ideal person, right?

Or perhaps, the perfect martyr.

Not all angry people express their anger with bellows and blows and malevolent housewrecking. Nice People (NPs, for short) swallow their anger, smiling as the caustic potion scalds their tongues. Swallowing anger doesn't make it go away, it just makes your stomach hurt.

Of course, not all idealistic, sensitive, loyal people are simmering cauldrons of unexpressed anger. Many are healthy, happy, assertive, and sincere folks who are exactly what they appear to be: nice people.

Happy nice people and angry NPs are alike in an important and superficial way—they're well behaved, civilized, mannerly. So when NPs get angry and stay angry, they still seem well behaved.

On the surface, anyway.

But underneath, hidden from view, chronically angry NPs harbor feelings that can eventually lead to trouble. We are fussy and thin-skinned, moody and resentful, insecure and withdrawn, critical and hard to please, unforgiving and vengeful, depressed and shy.

We feel unworthy and inadequate—and fear rejection should anyone find out what we're *really* like. Chronically angry NPs put on a good front for the world. We wear a smiley face to keep our negative feelings—our real feelings—hidden.

W*e're nice,* but inwardly we quake with fear and seethe with resentment.

Nice People attempt to bolster shaky self-esteem by "helping" people. NPs can't do enough for other people. We work hard, giving our time, energy, and money. We have special sympathy for underdogs and often involve ourselves with people who are depressed or misfortunate.

This may sound highly admirable, but in the context of the addictive family it can be as dangerous as dynamite. Why? Because the only way NPs can maintain any feeling of self-worth is by associating with someone who is sick or weak or more troubled than they are. In other words, NPs lose their sense of worth when the other person—say, an addicted spouse or troubled child—is no longer weak, sick, or confused. Without someone to "help," without someone to be better than, NPs feel inadequate.

Substance abusers and NPs form secret (unspoken) pacts with each other. It may go something like this:

He will drink a lot. She will lecture him about the drinking, cover up for him, keep the creditors away from the door, and hide the problems from the rest of the family.

He gets to keep drinking—in fact, may even use her nagging as an excuse for drinking. She gets to think of herself as a moral, superior person for putting up with this inferior drinker; plus, she gets the admiration of other people for "holding the family together."

The same pattern holds true for other forms of substance abuse besides drinking. The genders can be reversed, too.

Why do NPs behave this way? Why do we sabotage the people we love?

British psychotherapist Anthony Storr points out in his book *Human Aggression* that Nice People like us feel fundamentally unlovable, and thus, our sympathetic nature—our niceness—is merely superficial. We hunger desperately for love, yet we are frightened of appearing assertive or aggressive in any way, afraid we will be rejected if we openly ask other people to care for us or meet our needs.

Storr says we will submerge our own personality in that of the other person and will use our capacity for doing this as a kind of emotional blackmail. Our excessive concern over the other person's feelings is a childish maneuver to gain love, power, and a sense of self-worth. We will destroy the people we love rather than allow them to be healthy, free, and independent!

In short, here is another extreme of *anger disability*. Just as violent people learned to get away with mayhem, NPs learned they couldn't. NPs express anger through passivity, guilt-tripping, manipulation, and self-destruction.

An agreeable and pleasant demeanor can hide aggressive and hostile feelings. Passive people can be just as angry as violent people.

NPs can be of either sex, but nice women seem to outnumber nice men. Nice women are common in addictive families. The person most likely to be a nice woman is one who grew up with an alcoholic parent. Often, she marries an alcoholic. She may appear to be independent, but essentially she is a dependent person. She has an unusual capacity for putting herself in another person's shoes, for showing sympathy, for taking care of the needs of others. She is a friend indeed, but a friend in need—a natural caregiver who is often embroiled in the crises of others.

She's also frequently depressed, overweight, and manipulative. She has seriously considered suicide more than once. While her husband turns to the booze bottle, the NP frequently turns to the medicine chest, becoming hooked on prescription pain pills, diet pills, or tranquilizers.

What she wants most in the world is to be loved. But she's never learned how to say, "Hey, dammit, love me!" Plus, she's never learned to *accept* the words "I love you" when she hears them because she feels basically unlovable. No matter how much attention and love she is given it's never enough, never the right kind, never satisfying. Happiness is always a few inches out of her grasp. She is a casualty of the disease of chemical dependency.

Daughters and wives in addictive families often express their anger through dependency, self-sacrifice, manipulation, and self-destructive behavior.

On the surface, NPs are generally regarded as unusually kind people. They are able to sympathize with others and share their feelings. But their niceness, their self-sacrificial tendencies, can turn ultimately disagreeable.

As a typical NP, I will give you the shirt off my back, then criticize you (for your own good, of course) for not wearing the shirt with style. And because I went naked for your benefit, I caught a chill and ended up with pneumonia. "But don't worry"—cough cough—"you *(with your giant wardrobe)* needed the shirt more than I."

Do you see the pattern here? Our seemingly selfless acts of giving provide us with a power base, a base from which we can criticize, control, and punish. The recipient of our good will is, of course, obligated to return the favors by bestowing attention, affection, and blind loyalty upon the self-sacrificing NP.

But people being what they are, the recipients of all this generosity are often ungrateful. Worse: They can be downright selfish, mean, and awful! Does this mean the NP has failed? Not in the least! Because, you see, only a despicable coward would mistreat a person as giving, as considerate, as thoughtful, and as *nice* as the NP.

The NP wins again. Our low self-esteem is bolstered by the attention of those obligated to us, or by the knowledge that we are morally superior to the ungrateful dogs who have used us and then mistreated us.

NPs use gift giving, guilt, and manipulation to control other people. Sadly, these maneuvers ultimately backfire. The people we seek to bind to us, to make dependent, and to control end up resenting and often rejecting us.

Although feelings of moral superiority can give us a temporary lift, they can't keep us warm at night. NPs seek love and approval. We want other people to validate our self-worth because we don't know how to do it for ourselves.

We want control. Yes, control! Because we *fear* what we cannot control. We fear abandonment and rejection. Often that's what we get.

Why? Because, as Anthony Storr says, it is hard for anyone to love and respect someone who hardly exists in her own right. And while the NP's selfless acts may be appreciated temporarily, we can become intensely irritating because the gifts we give are never without strings. The target of all the gifts pays, and pays dearly, with guilt and anxiety and unhealthy dependence.

The NP rarely makes direct demands on family and friends. Instead, we drop hints, manipulate, sink into silence, display our pain, and withdraw our affection. It's as if we're saying *I'm suffering and it's your fault,* but we won't say it out loud, right up front, where people can deal with it.

The result? Family and friends feel angry and guilty while

grudgingly trying to give us what they think we want. We feel angry and hurt and demeaned because we *know* they don't *really* care about our feelings. Everyone loses.

Okay, this may not be a healthy or honest way to deal with anger, but is it really disabling? The answer is a resounding YES! This quiet kind of anger can actually be more destructive and difficult to deal with than outright violence.

Let's look at seven ways nice people are disabled.

1. *NPs are terrible money managers.* We spend so much money on gifts and "special treats" for friends and relatives, we often have to borrow money to meet our own basic financial obligations. If we are being fully or partially supported by another person, we may express our anger by running up huge bills for our mate to pay.

2. *Many NPs suffer from an eating disorder.* Unable to express our feelings directly, we may turn to food for solace. It may well be that behind every sweetly smiling fat person is an angry person struggling to get out. Overeating can be a way of quietly rebelling against critical and demanding parents or spouses. Unfortunately, our obesity often damages our physical health and self-esteem.

3. *Many NPs develop chronic physical ailments that prevent us from fully participating in family life or employment.* Angry NPs usually suffer from one or more of the following chronic disorders: obesity, heart trouble, ulcers, severe headaches, intractable pain (often back pain), adult-onset diabetes, weak spells, diarrhea or constipation, colitis, sleep disorders, fibromyalgia, chronic fatigue syndrome, and general nervousness. Sometimes there is no specific ailment, just a malaise that defies medical diagnosis. Because we are so busy

taking care of other people, we don't have time to take care of ourselves. We often shun doctors; or, conversely, we are frequently hospitalized, often for surgery.

4. *NPs are frequently depressed.* Depression is common among substance abusers and their children. Medical researchers believe some (or much) of this depression is biochemical in nature and related to heredity. However, in NPs this depression can be related to our feeling so unlovable and worthless, compounded by the disappointment we feel when friends and family don't meet our (unspoken) needs.

5. *It's not unusual for NPs to have sexual problems.* Although angry, an NP is too passive to tell a sex partner, "I don't want to have sex with you because I'm angry, riled, and upset over . . ." Women may show a total lack of interest in sex or may punish a partner by willingly (even eagerly) engaging in sex, and then show no pleasurable responses. This can be a way of saying, "See how inadequate you are. You can't turn me on."

In a man, passive anger may be manifested through lack of interest in sex or the refusal to ejaculate during intercourse. "I'll show you who's in control," he seems to say. His message is similar to the angry woman's. Of course, there are many other reasons for sexual dysfunction, but anger is a good possibility.

Extramarital affairs or promiscuity can also be a sign of anger against spouses, parents, or other authority figures. If this sexual activity brings little pleasure and lots of guilt, or if the sexual partner is merely a faceless blur, it's a dangerous sign.

6. *NPs sometimes threaten suicide or make suicide attempts to frighten friends and loved ones.* Such attempts are framed in a "See-what-you-made-me-do" attitude. In teenagers and young adults, females make 90 percent of

the suicide attempts, but account for only 20 percent of suicide deaths. These failed attempts may be a way of punishing and manipulating family and friends—or they may be an attempt to gain sympathy.

Although the NP may not really want to die, suicidal behavior must be taken seriously because a fake attempt can go disastrously wrong, ending in death or serious injury. An NP with a history of failed suicide attempts may also decide to go for the real thing in the depths of a depression.

7. *NPs can turn violent.* It may sound contradictory for an NP to also be violent, but it's not uncommon. NPs have such a compulsive need to control, to get their own way, that their frustration can reach intolerable levels. Their human targets are almost always small children who are dependent on the NP for care and survival. During adolescence, when the child is old enough to reject the NP through running away, withdrawal of affection, or turning to another adult for help, the physical abuse usually stops. NPs are also known for temper tantrums during which they break dishes, shatter glasses, throw things, and rip up clothes.

If you recognize yourself in even one of these seven self-destructive behaviors, you may be an angry nice person. If you see yourself in two or more, especially if you've ever attempted suicide or turned violent, you are suffering from an anger disability.

Can you be helped? Yes, of course! But you *will* need help.

Getting the Right Kind of Help

If you are a non-addicted codependent and not in Al-Anon—try attending some Al-Anon groups. Al-Anon can help you deal with your guilt and fear and with your need to control.

Al-Anon is listed in the phone book. Its members are women and men who love an alcoholic and who are struggling to find peace and happiness. They know what you're going through.

Besides self-help, you may also want to seek professional psychotherapy (individual or group). But listen, NPs are very resistant to therapy. We're so *good* at meeting the needs of others, so nice, so skilled at submerging our own personalities into those of other people that we can easily end up *giving therapy to our therapists!*

Listen some more. This is a serious problem for us: Our therapist and our group members may think we're absolutely wonderful—so nice, so giving, you know—but we don't get any help for our problems! Our ability to deflect confrontation by "helping" other group members and by being so attentive and supportive of our therapists *hinders our own recovery.*

So if you go into therapy, you must be brutally honest with yourself and your therapist. You might even take this book with you and point to this page and say, "I have this problem!" Forewarned is forearmed. If your therapist knows in advance that you are an NP, you have a better chance of getting help.

Because NPs are so insecure and suffer from low self-esteem and passive-aggressive behavior, we can especially benefit from assertiveness training and other groups that help us become more direct in stating our needs. Women NPs can blossom in women's support groups that nurture self-esteem and feelings of independence.

If you are overweight and suffering from compulsive eating, the last thing you need to do is go on a diet. You've probably already done that a hundred times. What you can do is join an organization that will help you understand and accept your eating disorder, such as Overeaters Anonymous.

Is your health bad? Are you depressed? More important, are you engaging in destructive and addictive habits? Do you smoke like a smokestack? Eat junk food and sugar by the ton?

Never exercise? Are you using prescription tranquilizers, pain pills, or sleeping pills? How about over-the-counter diet aids, laxatives, nerve pills, or sleeping pills?

Many of the health problems that plague NPs are lifestyle problems that can be dramatically improved with good nutrition and exercise. Most hospitals and HMOs offer free community education classes that can help us overcome destructive lifestyle habits. When we improve our nutrition and lifestyle, many of us will find that our attitudes and feelings also change for the better.

Dealing with an NP You Love

AA and NA can help addicts learn to deal with NPs who sabotage recovery, and Al-Anon can help non-addicted codependents. The best way for anyone to avoid an NP's sabotaging behavior is to learn to say *no*, gracefully, to any of the NP's attempts to take care of us. If we continue to accept money and gifts, if we allow the NP to lift the load of our responsibilities from our shoulders, we are heading straight for trouble in the form of guilt, anxiety, anger—and possible relapse.

Detaching ourselves from the grasp of an NP can be difficult and painful—for us *and* them. If you are the adult child of an alcoholic—for example, if your father was an alcoholic and your mother an NP—you would be doing yourself a big favor by getting in touch with the National Association for Children of Alcoholics. NACA addresses the concerns of women and men who are still suffering the after-effects of growing up with an alcoholic parent.

Adult children of alcoholics don't recover simply by leaving home. The wounds of the disease of alcoholism can last a lifetime if they are forever hidden from the healing powers of the open air and sunshine of understanding and acceptance.

There are also Al-Anon groups that focus on adult children of alcoholics, as well as numerous Adult Children of Alcoholics

(ACA) self-help groups in communities across the country. These groups are a valuable resource for those who still feel confused and emotionally upset by the experience of growing up in a family affected by addiction.

You can find out more about ACA groups by asking your local reference librarian to help you find library and Internet resources.

6

Resentments

Unreasonable resentment is one of the major emotional symptoms of the family disease of substance abuse. If getting clean and sober is our No. 1 goal in recovery, learning to let go of resentments is No. 2. It is one of the best things we can do for ourselves and the people we love.

Rule No. 2 for people recovering from the family disease of substance abuse:

Learn to let go of resentments.

The dictionary defines *resentment* as anger and ill will caused by a real or an imagined wrong or injury. (It offers *hatred* as a synonym.) Notice that resentment can be caused by real or *imagined* injury. That's an important point for us to remember. The blame and denial that keep us unhappily stuck in our addictions can also make us experts at seeing ourselves as victims. We tend to exaggerate imaginary wrongs committed against us. This exquisite sensitivity to injury cramps our lives and leads us to become guarded, suspicious, and jealous.

A Resentment Saga

A fifty-five-year-old construction worker and alcoholic, George was arrested for drunk driving on his way home from an out-of-town job site. It was Saturday night, George was a stranger in town, and the arrest was his third for DWI. Bail was set at $10,000.

He used his one call to phone his wife, Doris. "Get me the hell out of this stinking jail!" he ordered. "I don't care what it takes, but get me out!"

In a panic, Doris called their son, Steve. The two of them piled into the family car and drove 150 miles to reach George.

At the jail, Steve tried to bail his father out. He'd been through the routine twice before—a check for 10 percent of the bail and his father would be free.

"Sorry," the jailer politely informed him, "we can't accept a personal check for bail. We only take cash."

"But the jail in our hometown takes checks," Steve protested. The jailer looked at him coldly. "Cash."

"But it's Saturday night," Steve said desperately. "Where am I supposed to get that kind of cash money on a Saturday night?"

"Try a bail bondsman," he suggested. "But they won't take checks either." Summoning every ounce of courage, Doris called a district court judge at home at 2 A.M. to ask for a reduction in bail. "No!" the judge thundered, "and if you want to talk to me again, call my office at nine o'clock on Monday." He slammed down the receiver with a resounding crash.

"Please," Steve pleaded with the jailer. "At least let us see him so he'll know we're trying."

"Visiting hours are Tuesdays and Thursdays," the jailer informed him. Softening a little, the jailer said, "We have our rules. You can't see him or talk to him, but I'll let him know you were here. He'll be arraigned Monday morning. You folks better find a lawyer. This is a serious charge."

"Can't you let us see him for a minute?" Steve pleaded.

"No."

One look at the jailer's face told Steve it was no use arguing.

On Monday morning, George was arraigned. His wife and son were there with an attorney. Recalling the small fines levied against him for his other two DWI convictions, George refused the attorney's services. He'd decided to plead guilty and get the whole mess over with. That way he'd be home and in front of the TV with a cold beer by noon.

The judge advised George to consult with an attorney before entering a plea, but George stubbornly refused. He wasn't going to pay some shyster $3,000 to hold his hand in court. George told the judge he understood the charges and wanted to plead guilty.

"Ninety days in the county jail," the judge declared, "and a fine of $1,000."

Stunned, George was led away to begin his sentence.

On Tuesday, Doris sat opposite George, a glass partition between them.

"You bitch!" George hissed. "This is your fault. Why didn't you get me out of here? You and that no-good son of yours."

"We tried," she said. "But—"

"Don't give me that crap. If you'd gotten me out of here on Saturday night like I told you to, I wouldn't have pleaded guilty. It's your fault I'm in here. You and that judge. You probably cooked this up together to make me stop drinking."

"That's not a bad idea," Doris said angrily. "I wish I'd thought of it."

"See! You've as much as admitted it! You left me here to rot while—"

"Steve and I tried to get you out," she said, "but we didn't have enough money. We got you an attorney. We did everything we could."

"Like hell! You should have bailed me out."

"They wanted cash."

"You should have gotten it somehow. You could have put up the house for collateral, you could have—"

"It was Saturday night!"

"That doesn't matter. I counted on you to get me out of here and you let me down big time." He clenched his fists. "It's a good thing this sheet of glass is between us or I'd . . ."

Resentment Gone Ballistic

George's thinking was so clouded by anger and resentment that he sincerely believed his wife and son were to blame for his predicament. He imagined they had betrayed him. But he overlooked certain important facts:

1. He had been driving drunk.
2. His wife and son dropped everything and rushed to help him.
3. He'd stubbornly refused to use the attorney they had hired for him.
4. He'd insisted on entering a plea against the judge's advice.

The only person responsible for George's problems was George himself. He was caught in a pattern of anger, resentment, and recrimination, and his thinking was unreasonable and illogical.

For years he had bullied his wife and son. He'd trained them to jump at his command. They always tried to comply. As a result, the whole family revolved around protecting George from the consequences of his drinking.

Yet in his own mind, he was the victim. And his unreasonable resentments toward his wife and twenty-five-year-old son very nearly cost him his home and family.

Natural Consequences

Sometimes amazing things happen when people experience the natural consequences of their behavior. When circumstances prevented his family from rescuing him, George had to take the consequences: jail, a serious fine, and a period of enforced abstinence. While in jail, George dried out and started attending Alcoholics Anonymous meetings three times a week. He also talked at length with the jail chaplain several times. Eventually, George came to accept that he was an alcoholic. When released from jail, he continued to attend AA meetings. In many ways, his life improved greatly.

But he clung to his resentments against his wife and son. Spending time in jail had deeply humiliated him. He felt he had lost face among friends and co-workers. And in his mind, Doris had caused his humiliation.

Finally, Doris could no longer take his accusations, sarcastic remarks, and mean temper. She filed for divorce.

The shock of divorce papers woke George up. Fearing the loss of his wife of thirty-five years, he agreed to seek marriage counseling from a therapist who understood substance abuse.

The counselor told George and Doris that if they wanted to fully recover and if they wanted to save their marriage, they would have to straighten out their thinking.

Rooting Out Resentment

At its base, resentment always has certain negative, irrational thoughts. We need to figure out which ones are making us so angry.

For George, it was the irrational belief that his wife and son should somehow have rescued him from a situation over which they had no control. He further believed that, regardless of the obstacles, they could have gotten him out of jail if they had really wanted to.

He concluded, wrongly, that he had spent ninety days in jail because his wife and son didn't care enough to help him. He ran these thoughts over and over in his mind, until he made himself miserable and unbearable to live with.

Doris had unreasonably believed it was her job to rescue George whenever his drinking caused him trouble. She'd lied for him, borrowed money, made excuses, and babied him. In the process, she'd come to resent her husband for *making* her do these things. It had never occurred to her that she was actually *choosing* to help George remain a drinking alcoholic.

Now, *stop:* Think for a minute. Are you carrying around an unreasonable resentment? Do you run negative, blaming statements through your mind until you're so upset you can hardly sleep? If you're truly honest with yourself, you probably have at least one resentment that's causing you trouble. Stop right now, get a piece of paper and pencil, and write down your resentment(s). Write down the name of the person you resent, and then write down why you are resentful in one sentence.

Your resentment list might look something like this:

I'm resentful at...	*Because...*
My mother	She tries to run my life. She refused to loan me $500 when I asked, even though she had it. She gossips about me to her friends.
My neighbor	He reported me to the Child Protective Agency because I slapped my son.
My husband's ex-wife	She got a huge property settlement. She doesn't have to work and I do.
My husband	He forgot our anniversary.

Writing down your resentments is an important exercise. While it's easy for us to sit back and say, "Boy, that George— does he ever have a case of stinking thinking," it's extremely difficult for us to see our own unreasonable beliefs and thoughts.

We can't rid ourselves of our resentments until we *recognize* them.

Save your resentment list, because we'll come back to it soon.

Our Own Private Talk Show

There are many different kinds of therapy available today. Cognitive and rational-emotive therapy work especially well with individuals and families that have suffered from substance abuse. We can become unstuck from our past hurts and resentments if we practice changing our negative self-talk into positive self-talk.

These therapies tell us that the way we *think* directly affects the way we *feel*. If we want to feel better, it helps to examine the thoughts and beliefs that keep our negative feelings boiling.

Cognitive therapists tell us that we maintain and inflame our negative feelings through *self-talk*—the things we say and think to ourselves. If we suffer from resentments, we're probably dwelling on real or imagined wrongs committed against us. We have a tendency to let the embers of our resentment smolder for hours, days, weeks, months—even years after the initial event has passed. We may live in the present, but our emotions are stuck in the superglue of the past.

In George's case, the resentments were clearly unreasonable. But many of us suffer long-term resentment because we really and truly were done wrong.

For example, Monica's first husband had been a scoundrel. He used her and abused her, abandoning her and their young son when Monica was only nineteen years old.

Twenty years later, every time Monica and her second husband had a disagreement, Monica would say, "You're no different from my first husband. You don't really love me. All you men are alike."

In fact, Monica's second husband was loyal, generous, and considerate. He'd loved and supported her for eighteen years.

He was nothing like her first husband. Monica's resentment was unreasonable and unfair. Yes, her first husband had hurt her. But that didn't make it all right for her to punish the people around her for the next twenty years!

Monica needed to let go of her past hurts.

"It Isn't Fair!" She Cried

Addictive people and their family members suffer from another major problem that doesn't always look like it's related to anger, but it is. It's called *self-pity*. And like resentment, self-pity is caused by negative self-talk.

We feel sorry for ourselves because our family, friends, co-workers, lovers—the whole darn world—don't give us what we want, need, and feel we deserve. As we wallow in self-pity, we don't stop to ask ourselves if what we expect from our family or friends is reasonable.

Like George, we make an unreasonable demand and feel devastated when it isn't met. To complicate things, some of our demands are never even voiced. We just expect other people to know what we want. How unreasonable can you get?

Self-pity is anger, plain and simple. We're angry that life isn't fair, that it's full of hardship and disappointment. We see ourselves as victims tossed around by an uncaring world. We're strong believers in luck—bad luck for us and good luck for everyone else. And we're blamers. Who do we blame? Anyone handy: spouse, kids, Exxon, the environmentalists, the government, the extraterrestrials. . . .

Both George and Doris suffered from intense self-pity. George felt his wife and son had betrayed him. Doris felt unjustly blamed for something she had no control over. We keep our self-pity bubbling with self-statements like, "It was my husband's (wife's, parent's, child's) fault."

We think thoughts like these:

- I wouldn't be so tired all the time if my husband made enough money so I didn't have to work.
- I wouldn't be stuck in a job I hate if my parents had encouraged me to get a better education.
- I'd be more respected by my friends and have a better social life if my wife weren't fat and if she had a better personality.
- I wouldn't have had to spend ninety days in jail for my third drunk-driving conviction if my wife had come up with bail on Saturday night.

We're experts at this blame game. If we can't find a person to blame, we'll even blame God. Self-pity, resentment, and fault-finding are symptoms of the family disease of substance abuse. Part of our recovery process is fearlessly confronting these defects in our thinking.

Wait a minute! Hold it right there! Did I just hear you say, *Poor me, why is this all so hard? Why am I saddled with all these special problems?*

Well, maybe it's because the good things in life seldom come easily or without practice. It's true: We may have more than our share of problems. If so, that's all the more reason for us to put in the effort required to make our recovery work!

Consider the things that make you angry. Your sloppy stepchild, your lazy colleague, your insensitive spouse, the car that won't start, the snotty salesclerk, the boss who refuses to recognize your worth, your mother-in-law with her critical smirk. The list is endless. We get lied to, manipulated, fooled. We get insulted, ridiculed, used. Life treats us unfairly, dammit! Doesn't that give us the right to be angry?

Listen: Every single person in the world has similar (or worse) troubles to face every day. We are part of a huge mass of humanity facing the difficult problems of everyday life. Our problems are no more burdensome than our next-door neighbor's. People who look like they are sitting on top of the world have just as many problems and tragedies as we do. They just handle them better! (Or seem to. Appearances can be deceptive!)

Cope 'N Hope

Cope 'N Hope. Sounds like an oven cleaner. But coping and hoping—realistically—enable us to get out of the resentment fast lane. So we learn to cope with problems realistically, and we learn to have reasonable expectations about the people in our lives.

Having problems does not make us special. But we can *become* special—by learning to cope with our problems and angry feelings without destroying our self-esteem or trampling all over somebody else's feelings. We cope with our problems by learning to be responsible for our own happiness.

But, you say, your life has been nothing but one bad break after another. Your blood boils at the mere thought of the hassles that family, bosses, and so-called friends have put you through! They *make* you angry and unhappy.

Not so. We make *ourselves* angry by some line of illogical thinking. We blame other people for our own troubles. We "catastrophize," we make mountains out of molehills, we turn everyday irritations into major calamities. We get angry because we're thinking (partly unconsciously), "It's not *right* that Doris didn't get me out of jail."

Or: "It will be *unbearable* if Mary is late with the Bergstrom report. I'll look like a jerk if she doesn't do her job right."

Or: "It's not *fair* that I'm stuck with this crummy job and Joe got a promotion."

Or: "I'll *die* if Paul forgets our anniversary."

Let's stop for a minute. Analyze your thinking. Listen to what you're saying to yourself, the self-talk that's going on when tense situations come up.

We do have these kinds of thoughts and, indeed, they make us angry.

Our *feelings* of anger are triggered by our negative, irrational, catastrophic *thoughts*. This is the main reason we sometimes get into such a state over minor aggravations.

Here's a fact of life we had better not ignore: Recovering people can't afford to get into a state over annoyances. We can't waste our energy turning molehills into mountains. We don't have time to spin our wheels catastrophizing some little snafu into a major crisis.

Why not? Because we have *real catastrophes* to deal with. Things like broken families, damaged children, wrecked relationships, unemployment, bad credit, legal complications, and perhaps other problems.

We have *work* to do!—making amends to people we have hurt with our arrogant and selfish behavior, rebuilding a career left in the ashes of substance abuse, rebuilding the rest of our lives.

If we are to fully recover, we must learn to put the petty irritations of everyday life into proper perspective. We must take responsibility for our own behavior and stop blaming other people for our mistakes.

So what if Roy hogged the floor at the last AA meeting and you didn't get to have your say?

So what if Delbert was twenty minutes late coming home for dinner and the salad got soggy?

So what if somebody stole your parking spot?

So what if you got yourself in a jam and your spouse (parent, friend, child) couldn't or didn't rescue you?

For this, you're ready to make war? For this, you get resentful, bitter, and churlish? You'd risk your recovery by stubbornly clinging to that resentment? Life is too short and recovery too precious to squander serenity on petty grievances.

We can learn how to *cope* with our frustrations and

disappointments without becoming angry and resentful. And we can learn how to change unrealistic expectations into reasonable *hopes*.

First, we must thoroughly analyze away the illogical and self-defeating self-talk that's running through our minds. Second, we must practice (and practice and practice) using positive, rational, logical self-talk to develop reasonable expectations—*cope 'n hope*.

For example, ask yourself, "Will I *really* die if Paul forgets our anniversary? Is it really so awful if I have to remind him? Is it a crime for him to be absentminded? So what if I have to drop a few hints for him to get the message? In most ways, he really does try to be a good husband. I wish I didn't have to remind him of important things, but it really is just a teensy little flaw in his character compared to his good points."

The conclusion is that you won't die and it isn't necessary to create a torrent of unpleasant emotions about Paul's oversight. He probably feels bad enough already. And if he still doesn't remember after you remind him, well, you'd better find out what's really going on, instead of jumping to conclusions. *Talk* about your concerns.

By practicing this kind of rethinking—positive, rather than negative, self-talk—we can rid ourselves of old resentments and prevent new ones from forming.

Attitude Adjustment Time

Who's gonna make it better? *You are!* Let's take a look at some of the irrational thoughts that make us angry and resentful. Answer the following statements true or false.

True False

____ ____ 1. I have often been treated unfairly.

____ ____ 2. I wouldn't have so many problems if other people treated me better.

True False

<table>
<tr><td>___ ___</td><td>3.</td><td>I can't stand it if someone lies to me.</td></tr>
<tr><td>___ ___</td><td>4.</td><td>It really upsets me if someone snubs me.</td></tr>
<tr><td>___ ___</td><td>5.</td><td>If people behave badly, they should be punished.</td></tr>
<tr><td>___ ___</td><td>6.</td><td>It really ticks me off if things don't go the way I planned.</td></tr>
<tr><td>___ ___</td><td>7.</td><td>What happens to me usually depends on luck.</td></tr>
<tr><td>___ ___</td><td>8.</td><td>I've had so many unfair things happen to me in my lifetime that I'll never get over them.</td></tr>
<tr><td>___ ___</td><td>9.</td><td>There is no good excuse for breaking a promise.</td></tr>
<tr><td>___ ___</td><td>10.</td><td>If I have to ask my wife (husband, child, friend, lover) for a favor, it's not really worth having.</td></tr>
<tr><td>___ ___</td><td>11.</td><td>If people really care about me, they'll know how I feel about certain things without having to be told.</td></tr>
<tr><td>___ ___</td><td>12.</td><td>If someone hurts me in some way, I have the right to get even.</td></tr>
</table>

Answering true to even one or two of these questions suggests that you have a habit of blaming, resenting, or catastrophizing because of irrational thinking patterns. These kinds of thoughts are illogical and unfounded because they're based on the idea that we have the God-like ability to judge how other people should and should not be allowed to behave. Plus, we expect other people to be able to read our minds and behave accordingly. When they don't—boy, do we ever get angry! And resentful.

In the next chapter we'll examine more specific ways to overcome our resentments.

7

Conquering Our Common Conceits

In chapter 6 we saw how our irrational thinking and negative self-talk fill us with resentment. Resentments can thwart, undermine, and sabotage recovery. Recovery can also be hindered by *common conceits* generated by the strange notion that the world—and the people in it—should perform just so to meet our expectations and our needs.

The Big Book of Alcoholics Anonymous* aptly describes the alcoholic as an actor who wants to run the whole show. He or she wants to be not only the star, but also the director. This characterization applies to all kinds of substance abusers and their families.

Our thinking goes something like this: *If only we could get people to behave—to act the way we want them to—then we'd be happy.* When the show doesn't come off just exactly right (it never does), we tend to become angry, indignant, and self-pitying. We grit our teeth and fume. The muscles in our jaws tighten like clamps. Frustrated and angry, we hold others responsible for botched and bungled performances. Nitwits! Idiots!

---

* The Big Book is *Alcoholics Anonymous,* published by AA World Services, Inc., New York, NY. Available through Hazelden Publishing and Education.

If it weren't for the inept bunglers, we could be happy.
If they'd just listen to us and do what we want them to do.
If they'd only act right, for heaven's sake.

But they don't and they won't!

To expect others to meet our expectations is a *prime conceit.*
It's time to deflate it, and, at the same time, let some air out of
other cherished illusions and common conceits.

COMMON CONCEITS
I'm right and you're wrong.
I'm right and they're wrong.
I'm right and the whole damn world is wrong.

This thinking—*I'm right and everybody else is wrong*—is the
cornerstone of blame and denial. In turn, blame and denial
form the foundation for continued substance abuse, even in the
face of convincing evidence that our drinking, drug use, food
and exercise abuse, gambling, destructive relationships, or
other compulsive activity is harming our lives.

(Each of us has our favorite substance of abuse. If it's hurting us and the people we love, it doesn't matter much whether
that substance is a bottle of beer or a video poker machine. The
process of recovery is the same for all of us.)

Substance abusers and their families suffer from common
conceits on a grand scale. Dr. Bob and Bill W. recognized this
years ago. They completely understood the role that delusions,
anger, perfectionism, grandiosity, self-pity, and irrational
thinking play in keeping us from full recovery.

But how do we go about deflating the common conceits?
AA's Fourth Step—doing a fearless and searching moral inventory—is a wonderful example of how we can straighten out our
thinking. Taking an honest inventory can, indeed, puncture
some of our conceits.

But taking an honest inventory is not as easy as it sounds.

To better recognize and grapple with the common conceits, it helps to understand the "Wanting Sickness."

The Wanting Sickness

Much of our anger and emotional confusion can be traced to the Wanting Sickness. We want certain things so badly that we can make ourselves physically and emotionally sick when we don't get them. Some of our wants are tangible things that, with a little effort, are within our reach:

- I want a chocolate ice-cream cone.
- I want a new pair of shoes.
- I want to go to the beach.

Our most basic wants are intangible and abstract. Almost all humans have these wants even if we don't admit them out loud:

- I want love, approval, recognition.
- I want to be attractive, accomplished, admired.
- I want to be happy.

All these wants are absolutely normal. There's nothing wrong with wanting ice cream, new shoes, happiness, or love. But we get in trouble with our wants when we begin to expect other people to fulfill our wishes for us or when our wants are irrational and unreasonable. These are the conceits and the wants that inevitably lead to anger. For example:

- I want you to behave perfectly and to meet all my needs.
- I want you to make me feel happy and secure.
- I want you to love me no matter how I treat you.

Do you see the pattern here? We expect other people to follow a code of conduct of our design. We want them to be the source of our happiness and security. We want their love and approval regardless of how we may act. What happens when our expectations aren't met? We're devastated. "Not fair!" we cry. "Life isn't supposed to be like this!" With wonderfully warped logic, we accuse, "You're bad for disappointing me!"

And for every disappointment, we build a resentment. We're architects of venom and vengeance. Even though deep down, we may grudgingly concede that there must be a better way, *we'd really like someone else to make it better.*

There's good news and bad news. The good news: There is a better way. The bad news: No one else is going to make it better for us—*we make it better ourselves.*

We need to learn how to tell the difference between a reasonable want and an unreasonable demand. We need to identify and eliminate common conceits. Sound familiar? It should, because this is the message of the Serenity Prayer.

The Serenity Prayer is an all-purpose, all-weather tool for tightening, straightening, and calibrating faulty and malfunctioning thought processes. The Serenity Prayer never wears out, and it's guaranteed to work—if used regularly as directed.

If you haven't already memorized the Serenity Prayer, now would be a good time. It can have a wonderful, calming effect upon us if we repeat it quietly to ourselves whenever we start dwelling on the unfairness of life.

THE SERENITY PRAYER
God grant me the Serenity
to accept the things I cannot change,
Courage to change the things I can,
and Wisdom to know the difference.

Many of the things we want are totally unreasonable and outside of our control. We want what we can't have, but we lack the serenity to accept the limits of reality. For example:

- I want my life to be uncomplicated. (Reality: Everyone's life is complicated. The world is complex; the universe is complex; even the social life of termites is extraordinarily complex.)

- I want to be four inches taller. (Reality: I'm not going to grow any more.)
- I want to be able to drink like a social drinker. (Reality: I'm an alcoholic and I can't handle booze.)

Other wants are attainable if we work for them, but we get angry when they don't come to us automatically. We lack the courage to change the things we can. For example:

- I want lots of money, a nice house, and a fast car (but I don't want to find a job and work my way up from minimum wage).
- I want to be attractive (but it's too much trouble to fix my hair, coordinate my wardrobe, and exercise three times a week).
- I want to save my marriage (but not if I have to change, go to counseling, and quit drinking).

Some of our wants are vicious:

- I want to get even with you for hurting me.
- I want to hurt you because you didn't do what I wanted.
- I want to make trouble for you because I'm envious of what you have.

Stuck in blame and denial, we follow a predictable thinking pattern. When we don't get what we want, our first thought is *Whose fault is it—who screwed me over?* We're imprinted with the idea that if something bad happens, someone bad must have caused it, and that bad person must be punished to set things right. We think we have the obligation to get even, to settle the score, to let them know they can't get away with treating us this way. Thus, our resentments are born, nurtured, and energized.

How we handle our resentment depends on our anger style. A Bulldozer might yell and threaten; a Soulful One might sulk and seek quiet revenge. Whatever our style, if our responses are based on irrational thinking and negative self-talk, we spread confusion and bitterness, not harmony and understanding.

So, you ask, what do we have to do to change?

Practice Makes Perfect

Self-help writers sometimes promise that becoming a healthy, happy, rational person is easy. *They lie!* They know we want a quick fix, a way to remake ourselves overnight, an effortless way to become a more successful, less shy, happier, healthier, slimmer person with low cholesterol and a big bank account. All dreams and illusions. An old saying goes, *There's nothing wrong with dreaming if you wake when the bell rings.*

Listen: The bell is ringing now.

Transforming our lives is hard work. Getting our anger under control is hard work. Changing our irrational thinking and negative self-talk—again, hard work.

After all, if it were easy we would have done it a long time ago. But one of the most exciting and surprising truths about substance abuse is that *we can recover.* The most down-and-out crack addict can get clean and sober. Methamphetamine junkies can straighten up and become caring and honest people. Long-term alcoholics can find long-term sobriety.

Commitment and practice are the key words to improving ourselves—practice, practice, practice. Skimming through this book, or any other book, won't change our behavior. But we *can* change!

As we know, unreasonable anger and resentment interfere with our recovery process. Here are four things we need to practice in order to rid ourselves of the irrational thinking patterns that create unreasonable anger and resentment.

1. **Accept responsibility for our own behavior**. The Big Book says an alcoholic is an extreme example of self-will run riot. The same is true for all substance abusers.

   Because we always want to have our own way, we trample on the feelings of other people; then we're surprised when they retaliate.

   Although we blame them for hurting us, if we are really honest with ourselves, we can look back and see how our selfish decisions set us up to get hurt. We have to accept that most of our problems are basically of our own making.

   Accepting responsibility for our thoughts, feelings, and actions is the first step toward recovery. When we don't accept responsibility for our shortcomings, we become stuck—stuck in our anger, resentments, and unhappiness. A major obstacle to acceptance is lack of awareness. That can lead us to relapse.

2. **Become aware of our negative self-talk**. We're so used to blaming and catastrophizing that we usually aren't aware of what we're thinking and telling ourselves. Listen to your thoughts. You're probably making yourself angry with a lot of "what if" statements, like *What if this terrible thing happens?* Then the thoughts cascade through your mind in a riot of imagination:
   - I couldn't stand it if . . . happens!
   - What if she leaves me?
   - I'm going to kill him if I find out that . . .
   - What if grandmother finds out?
   - It would kill me if my daughter did . . .

   A lot of our anger-producing statements start out with, *It's not fair that . . .* or *It's not right that . . .* We seem to think we are the ultimate judges of what is fair and right, of how other people should behave. And when they don't meet our expectations? *Grrrrrrr!*

Stop! Go back and look at your resentment list (chapter 6).

How many of your resentments are caused by negative and irrational self-statements? For example:

- My mother has no right to interfere in my life. She's a control freak for hassling me.
- It's my rotten neighbor's fault that I got in trouble with the child protection authorities. He shouldn't have turned me in for beating my son.

Go through your entire list and make a note of the negative self-talk you're using to keep each resentment alive. This exercise is important because it helps us become aware of our irrational and negative self-talk. A little introspection on our part will often turn up a ton of similar statements.

Now, let's continue our examination of actions we can take to rid ourselves of our unreasonable resentments.

3. **Become aware of the anger sequence.** *Remember:* Our negative thoughts control our negative feelings. The anger sequence goes something like this:

We think (and say) to ourselves, *I want something.* If we don't get it, we say, *I'm frustrated because I didn't get what I wanted.* ⇨ Our next thought is, *It's an awful and terrible thing that I didn't get what I wanted.* ⇨ Next, we lay blame by thinking, *Whose fault is it?* ⇨ When we find a target for our blame, we think, *You shouldn't frustrate me. I deserve to get what I want.* ⇨ Then we become judgmental. We say, *You're wrong and bad for frustrating me!* ⇨ Finally, the justification for our wrath: *You deserve to be punished because you're bad!*

Net result? A whole lot of resentment.

We usually aren't aware of such thoughts when they're flashing through our minds. But if we sit down and think about it for a while, we can see that this is exactly what happens when we get upset about something. Maybe we don't use exactly those words, but we follow the same process.

But we don't have to. Instead, we can . . .

4. **Take action to derail the anger sequence.** With rational thinking and positive self-talk, we can derail the anger sequence before it derails us. We can stop resentment cold.

Denial: It's Not My Problem

We have all built up defenses to protect our egos from pain. This is normal. Substance abusers and their families have big problems with *denial.* We refuse to believe or admit we have a problem even when our lives are falling down around us. Denial is a hallmark of addictive families. It's what prevents us from seeking treatment when we need it because we don't believe there's anything wrong with us.

In denial, we say, *It's their fault—I'm the one who's been wronged.* There's our Common Conceit rearing its head again!

To rid ourselves of resentments we must confront our denial. But denial is a powerful thing. We can admit we are powerless over our addiction, seek help, clean up, and *still* be in denial. Oh, yes, we've admitted our problems with alcohol and other drugs, but what about the other areas of our lives? Does sobriety turn us into perfect beings, halos gleaming, with no further personality defects? Of course not. For us, denial is as natural as breathing. But we can overcome it!

Defiance: I'll Do What I Damn Well Want To

One of the major components of denial is *defiance.* Defiance is the will to oppose or resist. It is the contemptuous disregard of authority. In practical terms, it means that we hate being told what to do. *We* want to run the whole show. Defiance probably stems from what the Big Book calls our need to be in control, to be right all the time.

Because we naturally rebel against authority, we tend to keep ourselves sick, to really hurt ourselves, just to show the world nobody can push us around. And to us, authority figures can be just about anyone. A few naturals for this role would be our parents, the boss, the police, and, of course, our spouses.

But what about the doctor who tells us we have to quit drinking or our liver will fall out? "Sure, Doc," we say. Then later, at the bar with our buddies, we laugh and ask, "Did you ever notice there are a lot more old drunks than old doctors?" Some joke.

Suppose we do sober up and the same doctor tells us we have the beginnings of emphysema and we must quit smoking immediately. Do we quit? Or do we decide, as we light up outside the doctor's office, *I'll be the judge of whether cigarettes are hurting me (cough), and no old quack's going to tell me (cough-cough) how to run my life.*

That's defiance for you.

We'll kill ourselves with our bad habits before we'll let somebody else tell us how to run our lives.

We'll defy just about anyone—a counselor, a minister, our kids —who tries to help us. We'll defy anyone who tries to tell us what to do, even when we suspect—deep down—that there may be a grain of truth in what they're saying.

Depending on our anger style, we display our defiance in different ways. A Bulldozer might yell, a Lightheart might make a few sarcastic cracks and walk away. Bricks and Soulful Ones, with their quiet wills of iron, may be agreeable and cooperative on the surface. Their defiance is disguised. It comes out in the form of forgetfulness, lateness, incompetence, illness, or subtle sabotage. The point is that because of our tendency toward denial, we don't always recognize our defiance and irrational thinking. We continue the blame game! I'm right, we say, and they are wrong.

Challenge, Think Clearly, and Substitute

Stop: Let's take another look at our resentment list, this time with an eye not only to our unreasonableness and negativity, but also to denial and defiance. Let's start challenging our common conceits as well.

Your resentment list might look something like this:

I'm Resentful at . . . *Because . . .*
My mother   She tries to run my life. She refused to loan me $500. She gossips about me.

Thoughts about Mother: *My mother has no right to interfere in my life. (defiant)*

Challenge: She's only trying to help me. Is it so awful for my mother to worry about me? Don't I turn to her for help? Why, then, should I resent it when she tries to help in a way that's different from what I wanted? Do I perhaps feel defensive and guilty because I know I've behaved badly and have to ask her for help?

Thoughts: *She's a control freak! (insulting, blaming)*

Challenge: She's not so bad, a little irritable and demanding, but probably no more than I am. I've given her a lot of trouble and she's always been there for me. Is it a crime for her to worry and be concerned about me? Am I resentful when she nags me because she's often right? (*I told you so.*) Do I always do exactly what she wants me to? Are you kidding?

Thoughts: *She should have given me the money. (demanding)*

Challenge: Why? Haven't I borrowed money from her before and not paid it back? Why should she have to cancel her vacation in order to pay my debts? I'm always saying I want to be independent, so is it really so terrible that she won't let me be dependent on her for money? Am I resentful because I still want my mother to take care of me like she did when I was a child? Isn't that unreasonable?

Thoughts: *How dare she talk to her friends about me! (self-righteous)*

Challenge: Don't I talk to my friends about *her?* Haven't I criticized her endlessly to my sister and my friends? What am I afraid of? Am I afraid she'll reveal some of the bad things I've done? Is it so terrible for her to confide in her friends? Don't I do the same thing?

Use this process to challenge each of your resentments. Fearlessly attack all of your defiant, blaming, demanding, denying, self-righteous thoughts and substitute rational and positive thoughts in their place. Then practice, practice, practice! Get a pencil and paper. *Challenge, think clearly, substitute.*

An important note: At first this process seems cumbersome, but with practice you can learn to use these techniques automatically, without resorting to pencil and paper. But while you are learning, it's important to set your thoughts on paper where you can see them clearly.

And keep in mind that this is not a one-shot deal! Many resentments are so deeply embedded that we must challenge and rechallenge them over a period of days and weeks before we can *really* let each resentment go.

Don't forget to use this process for new resentments too. It's easier to prevent a bad feeling if we face it directly, right now, when it first starts to bug us.

Okay, you've got your resentment list and you're ready to go, ready to clean house and get rid of all your old, angry, hateful feelings using fresh, new, positive, rational thinking. But what about those situations where your anger isn't caused by a *fancied* wrong or injury?

What if you're being rational and positive all over the place, but the other guy is truly doing you wrong? What if your mother really *is* an unreasonable, demanding control freak?

What do you do when you need to express your anger and confront someone who is treating you badly?

We'll take a closer look at ways to deal with people who treat us badly in the next chapter. But first, let's take a Serenity Prayer break (fill in the blanks).

God grant me the Serenity
to _____,
_____ to change the things I can,
and _____ to know the difference.

8

The Ventilation Trap

"You go to hell!" Shawna screamed into the telephone. She slammed down the receiver and proclaimed, "That makes me feel better!"

"What's wrong with you?" asked Lisa, Shawna's roommate. She was baffled. "You just told off your boss and you seem proud of it. If you lose your job, you won't be able to pay your share of the rent, and—jeez louise—I can't afford to pay your share too. Why are you acting like this?"

"I don't have to justify myself to you," Shawna declared.

Lisa held up her hand. "Hey, I thought we were friends. What's going on? You've been acting so strange lately. You're so hostile."

"I'm not hostile," Shawna replied. "I'm *genuine*. I'm just being authentic. My shrink told me it's unhealthy to hold in my anger. I have to express my feelings, I have to ventilate my anger, or . . . or . . ."

"Or what?"

Shawna shrugged and said, "Well, you know, it's bad to go around with your feelings all bottled up. Especially anger. It can really be dangerous to hold angry feelings in. Anger just builds up and turns inward and causes all sorts of terrible problems like depression and guilt and anxiety. Even heart disease. When I get angry I'm supposed to get it out, not let it stay inside me festing. My shrink said I was depressed because I was turning my anger inward at myself. I'm just doing what my shrink told me to do."

Lisa looked at the ceiling for a couple of seconds, then cleared her throat. "Let me get this straight. Your shrink said you should tell your boss to go to hell?"

"Don't be a geek! He told me to express my feelings. He told me to be honest with people. He said they'd respect me more."

Lisa shook her head in disbelief. "What about your boss? What's she supposed to do with *her* anger?"

Shawna seemed confused for a moment, then hesitantly replied, "Let it out, of course."

"I don't think I'd like to work in a place where my co-workers yelled at me whenever I did something they didn't like," Lisa said. "In fact, I'd hate it!"

Shawna shrugged. "Whatever. You're so neurotic. I believe in letting people know how I feel. If they can't handle it, that's their problem. My shrink told me I'm not responsible for other people's feelings."

A week later, Shawna lost her job. Seems she'd offended too many people and no one wanted to work with her. Is it any wonder?

The Complications of Confrontation

The freewheeling, no-holds-barred expression of anger can cause us more problems than it cures. Shawna's therapist did her no favor when he told her to ventilate her anger. Why not? Because he gave her no guidelines for expressing it maturely and safely.

Shawna was a young woman, just out of high school, with very little experience in the world. Her father was an alcoholic and her mother abused both alcohol and methamphetamines.

Shawna had never had a good role model for expressing her emotions. When her therapist told her to express her anger and other emotions openly and honestly, he might as well have told her to express her feelings in Greek. It was a skill she had never learned.

Expressing anger safely and maturely is a learned skill.

Shawna's feelings — all of her feelings, not just anger — were important. They deserved to be explored and honored. But her boss and friends had feelings too. *We all have feelings.* Shawna's outbursts were not healthy expressions of anger; they were selfish and self-destructive tantrums.

We have no right to expect our family, friends, and colleagues to respond with therapeutic calm as we blow off steam. If we insult, ridicule, or humiliate other people in our quest to express our emotions, we're not helping ourselves — we're simply hurting others.

Stick with Serenity

Since the late 1960s, there has been a continuing trend in pop psychology that says we cannot heal from our past hurts unless we confront the person who hurt us. There's not one iota of scientific evidence to support this idea. There's also no evidence that expressing our feelings of anger will necessarily prevent depression, ulcers, guilt, or anxiety.

However, medical research shows that people who feel and express a lot of hostility experience more medical problems than people who do not go around feeling angry, aggressive, and imposed upon by the world.

Hostility is the opposite of serenity. *Our goal is serenity.*

Alcoholics Anonymous and other Twelve Step groups have a formula that helps addictive people recover. Nowhere in AA or Al-Anon literature will we find instructions on how to express our hostile feelings or how to confront those who have angered us.

AA hands out no bumper stickers that read *Confront Your Parents*. No way. AA tells us to take our own inventories. Our bumper stickers read *Live and Let Live* and *Easy Does It* and *Let Go and Let God*.

The philosophy of AA has helped millions of men, women, and teens to recover from addictive living. We would be wise to pay attention to the proven success of Twelve Step living. It works.

Yelling, shouting, telling someone off, hitting, or breaking things when we're angry may make us feel better momentarily, but more often than not these outbursts make us feel worse in the long run.

We feel worse because when we experience anger, numerous physical changes take place in the body. Heart rate and blood pressure increase. The muscles tighten. The digestive system changes in ways that can make us feel like we need to run to the bathroom. Adrenaline (the fight-or-flight hormone) is released. Blood sugar levels climb, then go down abruptly.

These physiological responses *can* lead to chronic health problems. But spontaneously releasing rage isn't the cure; it's part of the problem. Medical research clearly shows that displaying our angry feelings does not make us less angry. Instead, it nearly always makes the physical responses of the body—and our anger—more intense.

An uninhibited outburst of anger carries an additional hazard. It encourages the target of our anger to retaliate against us. Shawna learned that lesson the hard way.

As a tool for anger management, ventilating our feelings simply does not work. Some therapists recommend that we hit pillows or tear cloth to rid ourselves of our aggressive feelings. *But for recovering substance abusers, these techniques can be risky.*

If we're taking out our aggression on a pillow, if we're yelling at an empty chair or hitting a mattress with a foam bat—if we're really into it, really feeling our rage—then our adrenaline is pumping. Our body is experiencing the anger response.

One of the physiological responses to anger is fluctuating blood sugar levels. *Unstable blood sugar levels can cause recovering substance abusers to crave their drug of choice, be it alcohol, marijuana, speed, or chocolate cake.*

The founders of Alcoholics Anonymous knew what they were talking about when they emphasized *serenity* for recovering people. *The anger response increases craving.* Serenity reduces that gnawing sensation of craving that all of us have experienced. It's as simple as that.

Chill out. Stick with Serenity!

Remember: For addictive people and their families, anger is usually tied up with feelings of fear and guilt. Trying to untangle and separate these interwoven emotions is a painstaking task. So forget everything you've heard about the importance of letting it all hang out. It's not the best kind of therapy for us.

When we choose to enter recovery, it's vital that we choose a doctor, therapist, program, or support group that understands the complex nature of substance abuse. There are many gifted therapists and caring psychiatrists who know diddly squat about substance abuse. They can hurt us with their ignorance. We need the help of *substance abuse specialists.* Fortunately, there are treatment centers across the nation that specialize in treating substance abuse. Help is out there if we want it.

Avoiding the Ventilation Trap

If ventilating anger doesn't work for us, then what does? Certainly not ignoring the anger or suppressing it and hoping it will go away. No. We need to follow a step-by-step anger management plan. This plan has four basic steps.

1. We acknowledge our feelings to ourselves.
2. We identify what thought or situation is triggering those feelings.
3. We assess what changes, if any, we can make in the triggering thought or situation.
4. We take action.

One of the actions we may choose is to express our indignant feelings by confronting the target of our anger. Sometimes that is the proper and healthy course of action. But before we act, we need to closely examine our own feelings and motivation.

Upon careful examination, we may discover that our anger is caused by our own unreasonable expectations and negative self-talk. *Remember:* A normal part of substance abuse is a tendency to blame other people for our problems. A normal part of recovery is learning to let go of blame.

To find out if you have a tendency toward a negative or unreasonable attitude, ask yourself the following five questions:

Yes   No

____ ____ 1. Do you often feel that circumstances not of your making have deprived you of the good things in life?

____ ____ 2. Do you often feel your life would be a lot better if you had only married the right person?

____ ____ 3. Do you feel angry because life seems so hard and complicated and unfair for you while other people have it easy?

____ ____ 4. Do you attribute much of your present unhappiness to the mistakes your parents made in raising you?

____ ____ 5. Do you believe a person's happiness and success in life depend a lot on luck, good breaks, and connections?

Answering yes to even one of these questions indicates that you may have unrealistic expectations of yourself, other people, and the way life is "supposed" to be.

Remember: Our anger starts with an *I want* statement. When we don't get what we want, we start asking, "Whose fault is it?" And we always find someone to blame.

Our chronic hostility spills over into every aspect of our lives. We're primed to explode. If another car slips into the last parking space, if a salesclerk is rude, if our child eats the last spoonful of peanut butter and we wanted that peanut butter on our toast . . . it's . . . it's *outrageous,* an affront—absolute proof that nothing ever goes our way!

Every inconvenience, every disappointment becomes evidence of the unfairness of it all. And we let people know it!

Of course, this attitude makes us a pain to be around. Our friends get fed up with our constant grousing and complaining and negativity. Pretty soon, they start to give us a little feedback, maybe some constructive criticism, perhaps a dose of our own medicine.

We grow defensive. We find fault with *them.* Ultimately, our friends find excuses to avoid us. And then we can't understand why we always seem to get rejected. Quite simply, our hostility and negative attitude make us too difficult to be around. We've created a *self-fulfilling prophecy.* We expect the worst, so we react with negativity and hostility. Because we act like such pills, other people don't want to be around us, thus confirming our belief that the world treats us badly. It's a vicious circle; a circle of our own making.

Taking the Passion Out of Rage

Nearly a hundred years ago, William James, the father of American psychology, wrote: "In rage, it is notorious how we 'work ourselves up' to a climax by repeated outbreaks of expression. Refuse to express a passion, and it dies. Count to ten before venting your anger, and its occasion seems ridiculous."

This is still good advice. Unfortunately, refusing to express an emotion is usually confused with pretending it's not there. That's not what we want to do. We don't want to become repressed and tight-jawed, with brave little smiles pasted on our faces as we say, "One, two, three, nothing bothers me, four, five, six . . ."

While instantaneously expressing our anger is not an effective way of coping with our feelings, acknowledging our emotions is an important first step. Somewhere down the line, we may choose to appropriately express our anger, but first we need to *fearlessly examine* our feelings and motives.

It's important for us to recognize the difference between *expressing* and *acknowledging*.

To *express* means to reveal through speaking or behaving. When we express ourselves, we are telling or showing another person what we think or feel.

To *acknowledge* something means to own it or admit it as true. We can acknowledge silently (to ourselves), on paper (to ourselves), or through prayer (to a Higher Power).

Does the difference between expressing and acknowledging seem small? It's not, and here's why.

A typical expression of anger, for instance, might sound something like, "Hey, you jerk! What the hell do you think you're doing? Are you stupid or something? Either shape up or ship out! You hear me?"

This expression of anger is insulting, demanding, and accusing. It's also likely to provoke a retaliation: "Same to you, creep! Stick it where the sun don't shine!"

From there, the confrontation both escalates and deteriorates, with hurt feelings all around and very little solved. When we spontaneously express our anger without taking time out to analyze the situation and to calm down a little, we run a big risk of saying things we don't mean, of blowing small irritations out of proportion, and of feeling like an absolute idiot an hour or a day later.

The Four-Question Challenge

Because our emotions are complex, we need to pause as soon as we feel the first hint of irritation—when our lips are trembling with the desire to blurt out, "Hey, jerk!" We need to ask ourselves, "What am I really feeling?"

Our next question is, "Why am I feeling this way?"

Once we discover what is triggering our anger, we need to ask, "What can I do about it?"

The final question is, "What am I going to do about it?"

These four simple questions can help us change. *But remember:* The process takes *practice.*

When you feel yourself getting angry, STOP.
Ask yourself:
   1. What am I feeling?
   2. Why am I feeling this way?
   3. What can I do about it?
   4. What am I going to do about it?

Question 1 helps us acknowledge and own our feelings. It is an important step because it momentarily halts the anger sequence. When we focus on owning our feelings, we are prevented, at least for a minute or two, from laying blame on someone or something else.

Question 2 helps us identify what's triggering our emotion. It forces us to analyze the anger sequence and recognize irrational thinking and self-talk.

Question 3 helps assess our options. Are there changes we can make to improve the situation? What are they? Are we fighting to change something over which we have no control? Are we angry because of our unreasonable expectations and irrational thinking?

Question 4 asks us to make a decision. Now that we've analyzed our options, which one(s) will benefit us the most without harming other people? Will we be accountable for our own feelings and actions or will we continue the blame game?

In our using days, we were enmeshed in confusion, pain, and discontent. In recovery, we have the opportunity to create harmony and healing. The choice is ours.

You see, as we ask ourselves that last question, "What am I going to do about it?" we are choosing whether to sow discord or peace, whether to cling to our resentments or put them behind us as useless and destructive thoughts.

Again, we come back to an *I want* statement. If we choose *I want* to be right, *I want* you to do my bidding, *I want* to run the show, *I want* you to feel as miserable as I do, then our self-important attitude continues.

If we choose *I want* to make amends, to live and let live, to accept my own shortcomings, and to take my own inventory, then we are on the road to recovery.

But even in recovery, expect to continue having problems with anger and other emotions nearly every day of your life.

"What?" you ask. "You mean all this work and practice, and we're still going to have problems?"

Oh, yes, it's true. The magic of self-help has limits: People live happily ever after only in fairy tales and romance novels.

Trouble and strife and irritations will still come our way. Blue days will descend, resentments will boil, minor annoyances will drive us up the wall. We may even have a disaster or two.

But we can guarantee this: By practicing the Four-Question Challenge, we are in a better position to roll with the punches. We can face life head-on and with confidence because we're armed with serenity and courage and wisdom, ready to fearlessly challenge our conceits, negativity, denial, and defiance.

When Anger Masks Fear

The expression of anger gets complicated because we may not be owning or admitting the true reason for our angry feelings. For example, Rick had been arrested for drunk driving. As a result, the court required him to participate in an alcohol treatment program. He'd been making great progress, but suddenly he started missing meetings.

His counselor called to find out what the problem was. Rick exploded at the counselor, calling her vile names and blasting the entire system, starting with the unfairness of the police and ending with the incompetence of the alcohol program's secretary. The counselor assumed—wrongly—that Rick was drinking again.

It turned out that Rick's anger was hiding terrible fear. His beloved wife had been diagnosed with cancer. He was afraid she would die, just as his mother had died of cancer when he was a teenager. His fear was so great that he refused to talk to the doctors; he even refused to talk to his wife. He was paralyzed by denial. He couldn't acknowledge his real feelings, so he lashed out at a convenient target with the rage of his entire soul.

Fortunately, Rick's wife responded well to treatment. She called Rick's counselor and explained the crisis. The counselor then helped Rick come to terms with his true feelings. Slowly, he was able to grieve the loss of his mother and face the fear of losing his wife. Most important, as soon as he stopped expressing helpless rage and started acknowledging his true feelings, he was able to help his wife face her illness with courage.

I Feel Angry vs. You Tick Me Off

Acknowledging our real feelings is not always easy. Rick's behavior demonstrates the complex nature of anger. Temper outbursts often hide pain and fear that we don't want to acknowledge. We may be hiding from fears as devastating as

Rick's or from the common problems of embarrassment, social awkwardness, or shyness.

Fortunately, there is a skill that can help us. We can learn to make an *I feel* statement instead of a *you* statement.

You statements are accusing and blaming. They almost always make other people defensive and less likely to cooperate with us. For example:

- You did it again! You really piss me off.
- Why do you do such mean things?
- You don't care about me.
- You're selfish.

When we acknowledge our feelings, we make a statement. For example:

- I feel angry.
- I feel hurt.
- I feel guilty.
- I feel scared.

An *I feel* statement is neither accusing nor blaming. We are simply acknowledging we are experiencing a certain emotion.

Notice the difference between saying *I feel angry* and *You did it again! You really piss me off.* There's also quite a difference between *I'm upset* and *Screw you!*

I feel statements are not magic. They don't automatically guarantee that the person we're talking with will remain open and non-defensive. The biggest benefit is this: If we conscientiously practice using *I feel* statements, we may not react to a conflict by saying *You jerk! You creep! You rat!* and so on.

Learning to make *I statements* is the first step in taking responsibility for ourselves. We're owning our feelings instead of blaming something or someone else.

That will be an important skill as we face our next

challenge—learning how to safely and maturely *express* our feelings at those times in our lives when we simply must confront problems head-on.

Let's look at some ways to confront difficult situations with other people *and* maintain our serenity in the process.

9

Wrangling without Rancor

The Big Book advises us to avoid argument and retaliation, to shun rancorous wrangling for our sobriety's sake.

"An excellent suggestion," we say. "We agree wholeheartedly! But . . ."

But what?

"But how do we deal with the arrogant egotists and grandiose blockheads who seem to be lurking around every corner to subvert our serenity?"

There's the rub. So we rid ourselves of disabling resentments. We try hard to overcome our denial. We practice positive self-talk and make efforts to overcome our common conceits. And we use the Four-Question Challenge. We make progress.

But what about those times when someone close to us behaves in a way that is irritating, inconsiderate, disruptive, or even harmful to our recovery? Should we turn away, count to ten, and meditate on green thoughts in a green glade?

There are times when we simply *must* speak up firmly for our rights. If *we* don't speak up, nobody will. We have to let people know what's on our minds. We don't transmit our thoughts on a special "spousal wave-length" and our spouse doesn't have a built-in receiver that picks up random ruminations of discontent.

For example, Jennifer found herself fuming with silent anger. Her house smelled like a tavern and she blamed her husband, Calvin.

Calvin's older brother Mike had come to visit for a few weeks. Mike wasn't the most gracious of house-guests. He packed the refrigerator with beer, used the coffee cups for ashtrays, stayed up all night with the television turned up full blast, then spent half the day sleeping on the sofa.

"I could tolerate the late hours and the lounging about," Jennifer told her friend Alexis, "because Mike's on vacation and we used to do the same thing at his house. But all the beer and cigarettes are more than I can handle. Mike's so inconsiderate. And Cal won't hear a word of criticism about his precious big brother."

"Why are you making such a big deal out of it?" Alexis asked. "You and Cal used to party. I used to party right along with you. Why don't you lighten up a little?"

Jennifer sighed. "Lighten up? I wish it was that easy. Look. Even back then, when we were party animals, Cal had a serious problem with alcohol and I had a serious problem with nagging. Our life was unbearable. We needed to change."

"Well, maybe you're right," Alexis said. "But the change was so *drastic*. Cal went from party animal to Mr. Sober-sides overnight. I don't know exactly what happened."

"Don't you remember when Cal was in the hospital last year?"

"Yeah, he had a virus or something."

"It wasn't a virus," Jennifer said. "It was an inflamed liver and pancreas—caused by drinking too much alcohol. Cal was in terrible pain. For a while, I thought he might not pull through."

"You're kidding! I had no idea it was that bad."

"The doctor told us that Cal had to stop drinking. His life depended on it. So, Cal went to Alcoholics Anonymous and I hooked up with Al-Anon. He quit drinking and right away our marriage improved. But Cal's health was still bad. He also had serious lung problems from years of heavy smoking. But on his own, with no nagging from me, he quit smoking cold turkey. I've been extremely proud of him. But Mike doesn't appreciate the amount of effort Cal and I have put into our recovery. And Cal lets Mike drink beer and smoke in the house. I'm worried Cal will relapse—that's all we need, for him to start drinking and smoking again. I'm so angry with Cal for putting me through all this anxiety."

Alexis said, "It sounds like you don't trust Cal."

"I do!" Jennifer protested. "He's done so well."

"But be realistic, Jennifer. You can't expect Mike to quit drinking and smoking just because Cal did."

"But Mike is so blatant about it. I wouldn't mind if he put a beer or two in the refrigerator, but he bought two six-packs. And smoke! My God, he's a chain-smoker, and I don't even have any ashtrays. The least he could do is go out on the porch instead of smoking up the whole house. The doctor said Cal needs to avoid even second-hand smoke if he wants to stay off an oxygen tank."

"Have you said anything to Cal or to Mike?" Alexis asked.

"No way," Jennifer said righteously. "I'm not going to nag like I used to. Besides, if Cal really cared about my feelings, I wouldn't have to say anything. He'd understand and do the right thing."

. . . .

Jennifer had the best of intentions. She wanted to avoid her old habit of nagging. But she'd gone too far in the other direction. Instead of nagging Cal, she expected him to be a mind reader.

Too often we try to send our thoughts and feelings out in a kind of code. We drop hints. We grimace or give pained looks. Or we engage in passive resistance. None of these ploys works.

Worse, they can be *infuriating* to those we're trying to communicate with, because they're trying to understand us and we're playing charades.

Making *demands* doesn't work either because it's almost guaranteed to provoke resistance. Do *you* like to be ordered around?

We need to be direct, but not dictatorial. We need to stop playing charades about our feelings, stop trying to transmit important thoughts to people who can't read minds. Our goal is to be assertive, to speak up firmly—but quietly—when the time is right.

Jennifer had a valid complaint. Mike was an inconsiderate house-guest. But there was more to the story than Jennifer was acknowledging. She had always been jealous of Cal's family. She wanted to be number one in her husband's affections. When Cal failed to chastise Mike for drinking and smoking, Jennifer felt Cal was favoring his brother over her—and endangering their own recovery. But she was too embarrassed to say that out loud. So she fumed silently.

When we find ourselves becoming angry, we must sort out our feelings. Jennifer used the Four-Question Challenge and came to realize that only part of her anger was being triggered by Mike's inconsiderate behavior.

When Jennifer fearlessly analyzed her feelings, she had to admit that Alexis had been right when she suggested that Jennifer did not trust Cal. At first Jennifer wanted to deny this feeling. But it refused to go away. Her distrust was rooted in the old drinking days before Cal joined a recovery group. With the help of her Al-Anon group, she worked on accepting the idea that she had no power to control whether Cal would or would not drink again. Once Jennifer acknowledged that trusting Cal's sobriety was a problem for her, she was able to seek—and find—the guidance and support of others who had experienced the same fears. This didn't make her worry disappear, but it gave her a way to deal with it in a positive manner.

Finally, Jennifer acknowledged the biggest thing triggering her anger at Cal and Mike—jealousy. Jennifer often felt insecure and unloved. She'd felt that way for as long as she could remember. When Cal showed affection toward his parents and siblings, Jennifer felt diminished and left out.

After much thought, Jennifer decided it was unreasonable to be angry at Cal for loving his brother. It was unfair to be angry at Cal because he *might* be tempted to drink and smoke. But it *was reasonable and fair* to ask that her home be an alcohol- and tobacco-free zone.

Eventually, Jennifer got up the courage to voice her concerns about Mike's drinking and smoking. When she calmly asked Cal and Mike to respect her wishes, they astonished her by apologizing to her. Mike didn't drink during the rest of his stay and when he wanted a cigarette, he went outside. Mike hadn't understood the seriousness of his brother's health problems. Once he knew, he wanted to do everything he could to be supportive.

Of course, not all families are this cooperative, but many people will behave well if we speak to them openly, honestly, and with respect.

This episode taught Jennifer that her anger was much more complicated than it appeared on the surface. It took time and effort for her to challenge her feelings and her motives. To her surprise, she found she had three major issues bothering her. Two of the issues—distrust and jealousy—she chose to take to her support group. The third issue—inconsiderate behavior by her husband and brother-in-law—she confronted head-on, quietly, gently, and with love. She came out a winner.

Let's take a closer look at ways to effectively confront people who may be causing us problems.

Preparing for the Confrontation

If we must confront someone—if a confrontation is needed to improve a bad situation—there *is* a way to go about it that promises at least a chance of a positive outcome.

A positive outcome doesn't mean we always get exactly what we want exactly when we want it. For us, it means

- We make our point.
- We maintain our dignity and self-respect.
- We don't threaten the other person's character or self-esteem.

Our kind of confrontation is a well-thought-out, dispassionate, lovingly firm statement we make to a person we care about. During the confrontation, we have three goals:

- We want to point out how a certain behavior is causing trouble for them, or us, or other people.
- We suggest changes and state why the changes are important to us.
- When appropriate, we make a commitment to do what we can to make that change easier.

Gather your facts and be ready to present *specific* examples of the behavior you are talking about. Also have specific solutions to offer. (Of course, you've used your Four-Question Challenge to analyze your resentment!) Make sure your solutions are positive, reasonable, and attainable.

Remember: This confrontation is meant to be *a firm but loving statement*—not the opening bell for a fight. It may take all our rational coping skills to prevent a battle, especially since we can expect a certain amount of resistance, denial, and defiance from the other people. After all, they're only human.

The Confrontation

To make the confrontation, pick a time when the other person is not distracted. For example, it's probably not a good idea to try to seriously discuss a romantic problem with someone during the last quarter of the Super Bowl or on the way to a funeral. The other person's attention and emotions will not be focused on us and our concerns. (Maybe that's why so many of us feel the urge to argue at these times. Our conceits make us want to be the center of attention. Think about it!)

We also need to pick a good place, where we can have privacy and no interruptions. It's not a good idea to air your grievances at the company picnic or the Christmas dinner. Yet, people do it all the time. It's ineffective and usually causes a lot of embarrassment for the innocent bystanders.

Okay, we need to pick a *good* time and place, but don't wait for the *perfect* time. The perfect time never comes.

Now, get serious. If you mean business, let your face show it. You can't expect the other person to take you seriously if you don't *act* seriously.

Ted, sober for six months, handled a serious problem with his wife this way. "Mary," he said one night after dinner. "I have something to tell you. Can we talk for a minute?"

Ted's face looked so grim, Mary immediately turned off the television and sat down on the couch. Ted sat opposite her and said, "I'm really bothered by the beer you keep in the fridge for Ted Jr. and his friends."

"But they're over twenty-one," Mary countered. "Why shouldn't Teddy be able to have a beer when he comes for a visit? *He* doesn't have a drinking problem." Her voice fairly dripped with sarcasm.

Ted took a deep breath. *Stay calm,* he told himself. "No," he said agreeably. "Teddy doesn't have a drinking problem. But I do. I'm an alcoholic. And I know that means I could relapse.

Let's face it: I'm having a hard time facing that cold beer when I come home from work every night. I don't like having to struggle with temptation on a daily basis. I believe in 'out of sight, out of mind.' I feel like I'm being sabotaged in my efforts to stay sober."

"That's ridiculous," Mary replied. "You're being asinine!"

Stung, Ted paused for a moment. Then he thought, *It's a shame Mary's acting the way she is, but I can handle it.*

Looking Mary straight in the face, he said, "I'm asking you for your help, Mary. I need your support to stay sober. When you buy beer and bring it home, I begin to feel resentful. I'm afraid I'm losing confidence in your willingness to solve our problems together."

"You're the one with the problem!"

Ted swallowed hard and took another deep breath. *There's no need for me to get defensive,* he told himself. "Yes, Mary," he said. "I'm an alcoholic. I intend to continue attending my meetings and I intend to stay sober one day at a time. But I'm asking you to stop bringing beer home. It makes it more difficult for me to deal with my problem."

Mary sighed, "Oh, if it'll make you happy, I'll buy soda for Teddy. But you're the one with the problem, not me."

Ted smiled. *Poor Mary. She needs to save face by blaming me, but it's a start. That's good.* He leaned forward and gave her a light kiss. "Thanks for agreeing to help me, sweetheart. I really appreciate it."

Notice how Ted handled the confrontation: He stayed calm, stayed on track, and used positive self-talk. He also quit while he was ahead, resisting the temptation to harangue his wife until she agreed with him in every detail. He let her save face as long as she agreed to his two major requests. We can learn from his example.

Here are eleven points to keep in mind when we find ourselves in a situation that may require a confrontation with someone.

1. Pick a good time and place.
2. Be serious and firm, but caring.
3. State your concerns clearly and immediately.
4. Use specific examples.
5. Use *I* statements vs. *You* statements.
6. Stay on track.
7. Use rational self-talk to stay calm and reasonable.
8. Present clear, reasonable, and positive solutions.
9. State your commitment to solve the problem.
10. Don't insist on 100 percent agreement with your every wish.
11. Show your appreciation for cooperation.

The Ugly Argument

No matter how skillful we become at dealing with confrontations in a rational and caring manner, we will probably still find ourselves in ugly arguments. Why does this continue to happen even after we're into recovery? There are two main reasons:

1. We're not perfect people.
2. Nobody else is perfect, either.

Some people *like* to argue and fight. In the last twenty-five years many books and articles have been written telling people about the benefits of arguing. We've been told to *show our emotions.*

People are showing their emotions so much these days that we risk getting shot if we make a driving error during rush hour. Hey, it's dangerous out there!

As recovering people, we know we have special problems with anger. If we are wise, we will avoid fighting. Why? Because in unguarded moments, it's easy for us to slip backward, away from recovery and toward unreasonableness and negativity. Fights usually accomplish nothing, unless we consider name-calling, accusations, fault-finding, hurt feelings, and splattered egos worthwhile endeavors.

Fighting builds resentments. We become so intent on being *right*, and proving our opponent wrong, that we say and do things we are later ashamed of. Who needs it?

And listen: There's more than one way to fight. Bellowing and screaming is the most recognized way. The "silent treatment" is another. It's every bit as vicious as screaming.

If we keep our mouths clamped tightly shut while radiating hostility and slamming doors, *we're fighting*. Silent fights can go on for days, even years. It's a hurtful way to live.

Can we avoid all fights?

Probably not. The most important thing we can do to avoid unnecessary fighting is to *watch out for pressure times*. The worst fights happen when we are fatigued and under stress.

To avoid ugly fights, watch out for pressure times, fatigue, and stress.

When we're under stress, we start picking on each other; one thing leads to another and whammo! We're fighting. It's not each other we're mad at initially, but when the tire goes flat on the way to the family reunion and we're already late and the kids are fussing and the spare tire is flat too . . .

After the Fight

When the fight is over, when you've calmed down, *apologize*. Maybe you didn't start the fight, but did you do or say things to keep it going? Fearlessly examine your behavior and make amends where necessary.

Calming Others

Pressure and tension are all around. Those close to us can succumb to the stress, turning themselves into time bombs, waiting for the slightest provocation to explode! If this is *not* a chronic condition with our loved one, we know it pays to tiptoe around a bit until the crisis passes. But too often when we see aggression, we match it. Boom! The battle begins.

One of the things we can do to head off an angry confrontation is to *refuse* to fight fire with fire. While the other person is coming apart, *we model calmness.*

How do we model calmness? We relax. We keep our foreheads unwrinkled, eyes opened normally, noses not wrinkled, mouths not snarling. We keep our hands open, not clenched, our movements slow and smooth, our voices gentle. Such demeanor is unthreatening and unlikely to provoke an outburst.

It also helps to *listen openly and sympathetically,* even if the other person isn't making much sense. We don't need to challenge every word the other person is saying.

Listen, because this is important: Don't mock, grin, or laugh at the other person. Sometimes we try to lighten up a tense situation by adding a little laughter. This can be disastrous. Most angry people have temporarily lost contact with their sense of humor. If we laugh or tell a joke, an angry person will usually interpret our actions as ridicule. Laughter is not the best medicine when facing an angry person.

If the other person starts saying drastic things, it can help if we *reassure* him or her that less drastic alternatives exist and that we are willing to help find those solutions.

For example, Tom and Anna were both in recovery, but they faced a mountain of bills left over from their using days. Tom had been unemployed for over six months and now that he was working again, collection agencies were threatening to garnishee his paycheck. Several times a month, Tom went into a panic over money.

"We're going to lose the house," he'd rant at Anna. "We'll end up homeless.

"Why don't you divorce me?" he'd wail. "That way you and

the kids could get welfare and food stamps. You'd be better off without me.

"You've got to stop buying so much milk for the kids," he'd order. "We're going to end up out in the street if we don't cut expenses."

At first, Anna responded to Tom's panic over money with tears and anger. Anna's counselor suggested that she try reassurance instead. In reality, Tom's fears were blown out of proportion. Anna and Tom were working with a consumer credit agency to clear up their bills. Money would be tight for a while, but they were not going to lose their home. Tom was over-reacting.

Reassurance can be offered with statements like

- "It's all right; we've solved worse problems."
- "Don't worry. We can handle this one step at a time."
- "It'll be okay. We'll work it out."
- "We'll find a solution together."

One of the most important things we can do to calm another person is *help that person save face.* Nobody wants to end up looking like a fool, and a person will often cling stubbornly to a foolish idea rather than admit a mistake. We can ease the situation by not rubbing the other person's nose in his or her foolishness, by compromising, and by resisting the temptation to say, "I told you so."

In summary, there are four techniques for calming angry people:

- model calmness
- listen openly and sympathetically
- be reassuring
- help them save face

Admitting Defeat

Linda did everything right and it almost drove her crazy.

"I didn't know what was wrong with me," Linda admits. "I took my inventory; I worked on letting go of my resentments; I practiced rational thinking; I went into therapy. Still, my family life was miserable!"

Linda lived with her husband, Phil, and his fourteen-year-old daughter, Pam, from a previous marriage. Linda and Phil had been married for three years before Pam came to live with them. The girl's mother had given up on her.

"Pam was a handful," Linda says. "But Phil made it clear that he wanted me to be Pam's friend as well as her stepmother. It was a disaster from the start! Pam was surly and disobedient and into drugs. Phil refused to discipline her. I guess he suffered from the divorced-father 'guilts.' Anyway, the situation went from bad to worse. I work full time, but neither Phil nor Pam would help with the housework, which really infuriated me because before Pam came Phil did share the chores. After a few months, I was exhausted."

Linda's counselor suggested that Linda set up a family conference, a structured confrontation where Linda could express her concerns clearly and ask Phil and Pam to take on their fair share of the chores. The confrontation went off beautifully.

"Okay, okay, you're right," Phil agreed.

"Sure, whatever you say," Pam sighed.

But nothing changed. Another family conference, more promises of cooperation. No follow-through. When Linda tried to discuss Pam's obvious drug use, both Phil and Pam stomped angrily out of the room, swearing at Linda as they went.

"Phil and I were fighting all the time," Linda remembers. "Pam was totally out of control and no matter what I did, nothing changed!"

After three years of misery, Linda divorced Phil. "I didn't

leave because of Pam," Linda says. "I would have stuck it out all the way if Phil had been willing to work with me, but he refused family therapy and he refused to help Pam with her drug problem. He didn't seem to notice that his daughter was going down the tubes in front of our eyes. Pam's in prison now, for armed robbery. I visit her occasionally, but I never see Phil."

Linda faced a heartbreaking reality: *Some people just won't change.* They make promises, but they have no intention of changing and they don't care whether we like it or not.

If their annoying behavior is something minor, say, they *never* hang up their clothes or they put empty milk cartons back in the refrigerator, may we suggest you simply *lower your expectations.*

But what if it's something major? Like drug use or gambling or physical abuse. What then?

Ann Landers, the advice columnist, poses this question to readers contemplating divorce: *Decide if you'd be better off with or without the spouse.*

If the problem threatens your health, safety, or recovery, and if, after a loving confrontation, the other person is unwilling to start making some changes, you may not be able to continue the relationship, even if it is a family one.

The situation is heartbreaking and real. The decision is not to be made in the heat of anger. Unfortunately, even our best efforts can't fix every relationship. We can only hope that our coping skills can carry us through the painful transition in one piece.

The Limits of Reason

The story is told of a young man who believed he was dead. His psychiatrist finally hit upon a logical, rational way to convince the young man that he was very much alive. He taught the young man to tell himself over and over, "Dead men don't bleed, dead men don't bleed."

After the young man had practiced this bit of rational self-talk for a couple of weeks, the psychiatrist pulled out a pin and drew blood from the young man's finger. The young man gazed in astonishment and wonder as droplets of blood formed on his fingertip.

"Now what do you say?" the psychiatrist asked triumphantly.

"By God!" the young man exclaimed. "Dead men *do* bleed!"

The point of the story is that rational coping skills have their limits. We can be paragons of rationality and still come up against the unreasonable and illogical behavior of our friends, colleagues, and families.

We can't win 'em all.

10

Beyond the Serenity Prayer

Let's say we've made some clear progress: We've really begun to accept that there are some things we can't change. We've mustered up the courage to begin changing some of the things we can. And we're slowly acquiring the wisdom to know the difference. But there's one more step beyond the Serenity Prayer.

Forgiveness

To err is human, goes the old saying, and to forgive is divine. Unfortunately, a divine attitude seldom comes easily. We often carry grudges openly and relentlessly.

Hallie is a good example of someone who learned about forgiveness a little too late. She is a courageous woman who has conquered many addictions. First diet pills, then alcohol, then compulsive spending. In her mid-thirties, she struggled with a life-long problem of compulsive eating. Not that you could tell by looking at her. She wore size twelve. But she'd always wanted to be a size eight—an unrealistic goal for a woman with her unmistakable curves and large bone structure.

Since adolescence, her life had revolved around public efforts to shed pounds, followed by ravenous eating when she was alone. Her food addiction had led directly to her first addiction to diet pills.

Hallie blamed her problems on her father, Herb. She hated him. Or so she said.

Herb was a reserved, no-nonsense type of man who had never understood his eldest daughter's emotional intensity, her passion for living, her moods. And Hallie had never understood her father.

He disapproved of much of her behavior and said so. Frequently he urged Hallie to "straighten up and fly right." That was his favorite phrase. Hearing it drove Hallie up the wall. She didn't know why he couldn't accept her and love her just as she was.

Hallie felt like her father had always tried to buy her off. He'd given her material things—fashionable clothes, a small car, and her college education. But he was a workaholic who spent little time with his family, and, except for material things, he'd ignored Hallie while she was growing up.

Seven years after she'd left home, Hallie was living in a city far away from her parents. But she still keenly resented the emotional neglect she'd suffered as a child. She felt constricted and inadequate, cheated and rejected, and she felt it was her father's fault. Her therapist seemed to confirm Hallie's suspicions.

"How did you feel when your father ignored you?" the therapist asked.

"Confused," Hallie replied, "and depressed. I wanted him to show his love; I wanted his approval."

"You felt like he disapproved of you, then. It must have made you feel alone."

"Yes!" Tears brimmed in Hallie's eyes as she remembered the way her father used to shake his head and roll his eyes when she talked about her dreams and plans. "He never listened to me. And he always made me feel stupid!"

"Stupid?"

"Yes," Hallie said bitterly. "Stupid and weak and powerless. And I still feel that way."

"Give me an idea how it makes you feel now, how it affects your life."

"Oh, God, I'm so embarrassed," Hallie said. "Here I am, thirty-four years old, and I still feel like a kid! I needed him to show me he understood and cared about me. But he didn't."

"It sounds like you feel he really let you down, like he cheated you."

"That's it exactly," Hallie said. "I was cheated. And I want him to know it. I want to tell him. But I'm scared."

"It's a scary thing to do, to let your father know your real feelings."

Through several more therapy sessions, Hallie came to believe that the only way she could rid herself of her hate and despair was to face her father, not as a child full of fear, but as an adult. She wouldn't let him intimidate her this time either. She wouldn't back down; she'd say exactly how his coldness and neglect had hurt and damaged her.

It wasn't long before the perfect opportunity presented itself. Her father was retiring in a month, due to his failing health, and a big family party was planned. She could kill two birds with one stone by using her vacation time to visit her family and have it out with her dad.

The confrontation went according to plan. She blasted him with the facts. And when he tried to change the subject, she kept at him, throwing his faults in his face, documenting in painstaking detail the neglect she'd suffered, until he finally broke down. He wept.

For the first time in her life, Hallie saw her father show real emotion. She felt triumphant. Every resentment had been aired; every last bit of her wrath had been vented. Her father— her big, strong, emotionless father—had finally been defeated.

Hallie's mother was furious. "How dare you speak to your father that way! After all he's done for you, and in his condition!"

"Don't worry, Mom," Hallie said confidently. "Now that everything's out in the open, we can deal with it honestly. We can have a real relationship as equals now." *And*, Hallie mused with silent satisfaction, *you're next on my list, Mom.*

The next day, Hallie flew back home feeling a sense of accomplishment and pride. But the feeling was short-lived. Three weeks later her father was dead. His illness had been much more serious than Hallie had been willing to see.

Hallie was stunned. Her dad had always seemed so powerful and indestructible. Denial and resentment had blinded her. The dream of all the good things to come, the fantasy of a real relationship with her father, lay in ashes and dust.

Hallie made an important discovery too late: She had loved her father—really loved him. But in her single-minded pursuit of revenge, she had neglected to let him know of her love and gratitude. She had turned bitter and selfish. Hallie's last memory of her father, and her father's last memory of her, was one of ugliness, recrimination, and persecution.

Several years later, Hallie still struggles with her guilt and grief. She would do anything if she could turn back the clock to that fateful day and change history.

A friend asked Hallie, "If you had the chance to do it over again, with what you know now, what would you say to your father?"

Hallie thought hard for a moment, then said, "I would go to him, put my arms around him, and say, 'I love you, Dad. I know you did the best by me that you could. Let's let bygones be bygones.'" Hallie sighed. "And if I still felt resentment? I'd go out to the highest hill and rail at the sky until I had no more strength left in me; then I'd drop to my knees and ask my Higher Power to give me the courage and wisdom to forgive my father for whatever he had done to hurt me. I'd spend my time trying to make myself into the person I want to be, instead of trying to re-make my father into the fantasy Dad that I desired. I'd do all the stuff I learned in my Twelve Step programs, but this time I'd work the whole program instead of just picking out the easy parts. That's what I'd do if I had the chance. And that's what I am doing, one day at a time. I can't undo the past, but I don't have to make the same prideful mistakes again."

Forgiving Sins of Omission

Hallie's father had been guilty of what are called sins of omission. He had not beaten his daughter, or verbally abused her, or starved her, or thrown her out into the street. His mistakes were much less tangible—he had failed to understand Hallie's secret needs. He did what most good fathers of the past did. He worked hard to provide his family with a nice home, good food, and a decent living. Until recently, men weren't expected to nurture; they provided. Herb provided, and in the process he made some mistakes. *All parents make mistakes in raising their children.*

But somehow, some way, we've reached a point in our society where many adults have come to believe that they were cheated if their parents didn't provide a *Leave It to Beaver* or *Brady Bunch* home life. These expectations of parental perfection are totally unrealistic and can only lead to feelings of unhappiness, deprivation, and anger.

None of us is a perfect being; we will all make mistakes. Much of our anger is directed at people who weren't there when we needed them, people who disappointed us or let us down because they were so involved with their own concerns that *they failed to recognize what we needed from them.*

Listen: Sins of omission happen in every family, every marriage, every friendship. We cannot escape them! By forgiving those who have hurt us through sins of omission, we free ourselves from the burden of bitterness, hate, and isolation. While blame is one of the worst of human behaviors, forgiveness is one of the best. Forgiveness frees us to love again.

And on the practical side, it's a lot easier to discuss

problems with people we care about if we're not brimming over with past hurts and unresolved anger. In general, people are more willing to listen to us if they don't feel like we're about to attack or criticize them.

Think about it: Do you like being criticized? Wouldn't you like to be forgiven for your past blunders and mistakes? Addiction causes so much pain. That's a fact. In recovery, forgiveness is the key to renewal and serenity.

Self-Statements That Help Us Forgive Sins of Omission

- I know _____ did the best he or she could.
- Everyone makes mistakes. I know _____ didn't mean to hurt me.
- That was then, and this is now. Let's start over from today.
- Grant me the strength to forgive _____ for what he or she did to harm me.
- I forgive _____. My heart is filled with love.

Forgiving Sins of Commission

What about people who have gone out of their way to harm us? People who acted against us purposefully and with the full intent to cause us trouble? Or the ones who just didn't care whether or not we were hurt? Do we forgive those people?

Yes, if the act of forgiveness will relieve us of the burden of hate that is poisoning our recovery. We don't have to like those people, the way they acted, or what they did to us. We don't have to let them back into our lives. The Big Book suggests we realize that perhaps the people who wronged us were sick, suffering from a spiritual illness. It suggests we show them the same pity we would show sick people.

So, it is *wise* to forgive, but we don't have to forget. By not forgetting what these people did, we can avoid trouble in the future.

It is *unwise* to trust people who have proven to be untrustworthy. Forgiving others does not mean we have to trust them again. To do so could be foolish and even dangerous on our part.

* * * * * * * * *

Alan had trusted his brother to invest a considerable sum of money in the stock market. Instead, the brother used Alan's money at the race-track and lost it all. Alan found the strength to forgive his brother, but he never again gave his brother money to invest.

* * * * * * * * *

As a child, Christine had been sexually abused by her father. After much therapy, she found the strength to forgive him because the act of forgiveness set her free to get on with her life. She no longer felt victimized and vulnerable. Because she no longer felt like her father's victim, he no longer had emotional power over her.

She didn't pretend that everything in their relationship was just fine. She detached herself from his spiritual illness, spending very little time with him and refusing to allow him to be alone with his grandchildren.

Most important, she broke the code of silence. With the help of a therapist, she told her mother what had happened. The therapist's support was crucial because Christine's mother was devastated by the news. Christine's lovingly firm confrontation resulted in her father seeking in-patient treatment.

Unlike Hallie, Christine did not confront her parents in order to gain a feeling of power or to wreak revenge. Christine's motives were unselfish: She didn't want other children to be victimized by her father's illness.

Some of Christine's friends tell her she was wrong to forgive her father. They think that lets him off the hook. Christine disagrees. "I've come to accept that my father has a spiritual illness," she explains. "That acceptance allows me to forgive him. But it also warns me not to trust him. He's still sick. He still can't be trusted. I forgave him because my anger and hatred toward him was ruining *my* life. He ruined my childhood. I don't have to give him the rest of my life too. Since I forgave him, I feel detached from him. I feel free."

•••••••••

Bob quit drinking on his own, but he remained ill-tempered, pessimistic, and argumentative. Every holiday season, he visited his parents and created chaos by picking fights with his grandparents and by using deplorable language at the dinner table in front of his young nieces and nephews. Every Thanksgiving and Christmas turned into a nightmare.

Bob's parents loved him dearly, but they banned him from attending family gatherings until he agreed to seek treatment for his problems. They told him they would welcome him again if he would attend Alcoholics Anonymous meetings or some other treatment program. Bob refused.

His parents started attending Al-Anon meetings. Bob's mother says, "At first, I was so angry at Bob for spoiling our holidays that I wanted to disown him. But he's still my son and I love him. Al-Anon helped me realize that I wasn't a victim of Bob's bad behavior; I was a volunteer. I was the one who had always begged him to spend holidays with us. When Bob finally gets help for his problems—and mark my words, I said *when*, not *if*—he'll be welcomed home. Forgiveness allows me to love my son, even if I can't live with the way he acts. I have faith that he'll eventually choose recovery. His father and I will be there for him when he makes that choice."

•••••••••

Julie involved herself in local politics. When she challenged the local power structure, she found herself the target of a smear campaign. "People I trusted and respected said terrible things about me, things that were absolute lies. Then they'd look at me innocently and deny they'd done it. They told me they were my friends; they really played up to me, and I kept falling for it. In the meantime, they were going behind my back and doing everything they could to ruin my credibility. This wounded me deeply.

"For a while, I felt horribly bitter and said I'd never trust anyone again as long as I lived. But when I acted like that, it made people think that maybe I really was the terrible character they'd heard about. I decided the only way to save my reputation and my sanity was to just get over it. I needed to stop thinking about what they'd done to me. To do that I had to accept that they'd lied about me. I had to acknowledge to myself how much it hurt me, and then I had to let it go.

"But I don't want to be suckered in again by people who only pretend to be my friends. I need to remember that these people are not worthy of my trust. So, I put a sign next to my bathroom mirror that reads:

To Err is Human.
To Forgive, Divine.
To Forget, Foolhardy.

"Whenever I hear some new lie my former friends have spread about me, I do my best to forgive. I've had a number of people ask me why I don't get angry and bitter—they wonder why I don't fight fire with fire. But I think that by forgiving the people who hurt me, and who go on trying to hurt me, I save myself a lot of stress. Forgiveness means nothing to the people who've hurt me. They don't care. *But I care.* My life is so much better since I've learned to stop hating my adversaries. Their lies have actually made me stronger, more centered."

Forgiving Does Not Mean Forgetting

Most people have a difficult time with the idea of *forgiving* without *forgetting*.

"I just don't get it," Patty said. "If I forgive someone, doesn't that mean that I have to act like nothing ever happened? Don't I have to let them back into my life and risk getting hurt all over again?"

Not necessarily.

Forgiveness is something we do to heal our own pain. It's a way of letting go of past hurts. It doesn't mean we have to give someone who has hurt us a chance to do it all over again. Why would we want to allow someone the opportunity to brutalize us again, or humiliate us, sexually abuse us, rip us off, or hurt our children?

Some People Can't Be Trusted

However, many people—especially people who are actively participating in a recovery program—deserve a second chance. Addiction makes good people behave badly. With recovery, we have the chance to discover a person's true colors—often a pleasant surprise!

If we forgive people who have hurt us and if we want them to remain an important part of our lives, then we can't go around throwing their past mistakes in their faces every time we feel angry.

Forgiving, without forgetting, means we no longer pretend that everything is okay if it's not. That may lead us to therapy or a support group to help us let go of our anger and fear. Sometimes we can't get un-stuck from the past without the wisdom and guidance of others who understand our pain.

The poet Alfred, Lord Tennyson described an attitude

toward forgiveness that is often displayed by those of us who remain stuck in the past.

> Forgive! How many will say "forgive," and find
> A sort of absolution in the sound
> To hate a little longer.

Recovery means letting go of hatred.

· · · · · · · · ·

The late Reverend Lawrence Martin Jenco knew about forgiveness. Jenco, a Roman Catholic priest, was kidnapped by terrorists in Beirut, Lebanon, in January 1985. He was held hostage in a 12-by-15-foot room for eighteen months.

Jenco wrote a book about his experience, *Bound to Forgive: The Pilgrimage to Reconciliation of a Beirut Hostage.* When he passed away in 1996, the *Oregonian* newspaper reported that he held no animosity toward those who held him captive for a year and a half, despite the fact that his treatment was sometimes brutal and terrifying. He forgave his captors. But he did not forget.

Jenco said, "I don't believe that forgetting is one of the signs of forgiveness. I forgive, but I remember. I do not forget the pain, the loneliness, the ache, the terrible injustice. But I do not remember to inflict some future retribution."

The wisdom of this godly man speaks to all people who have suffered.

Forgiving Ourselves

How terribly we suffer from the unspeakable shame of our own sins! We have all made mistakes. We've said and done things we regret; we've connived and hurt people who have trusted us. Yes! We each carry our own secret store of sorrow and guilt.

If we can forgive others, can we not forgive ourselves? Are we not deserving of the same tolerance we show others?

Forgiveness is an act of healing. If we look beyond our guilt, recognize our wrongs, and work fearlessly to correct our mistakes, then we have the right to forgive ourselves for both our sins of omission and commission. If we are unable to forgive ourselves for the wrongs we have committed in the past, we may be condemning ourselves to a lifetime of fear and guilt.

A *warning:* Forgiveness does not grant us the right to continue our destructive ways.

Forgiveness grants us the freedom to heal, to start afresh, to make amends, to love.

Forgiveness is not the end, it is the beginning.

Index

A

Addiction, 5–6, 13. *See also* Recovery; Relapse
  domestic violence and, 34–35
  as family disease, 17–19
Adult children of alcoholics, 20, 50, 57–58
Adult Children of Alcoholics (ACA), 57–58
Al-Anon, 55–56, 57, 87, 120
Alcoholics Anonymous (AA), 41, 57, 87–88
  Fourth Step (moral inventory), 73
Alcoholics Anonymous (the Big Book), 72, 78, 80, 98, 118
Amends, making, 107
Anger. *See also* Anger styles; Expression of anger
  craving for addictive substances and, 89
  determining level of problems with, 10–12
  four-step management plan, 89–94, 101–2
  health problems related to, 53–54, 87, 88
  normality of, 4, 8, 13
  physiological response to, 88, 89
Anger sequence, 79–80

Anger styles, 23–58, 77
  the Brick, 26–28, 81
  the Bulldozer, 25–26, 77, 81
  defiance and, 81
  the Lightheart, 29–30, 81
  of Nice People (NPs, codependents), 48–58
  the Soulful One, 28–29, 77, 81
  violent behavior (*see* Violent behavior)
Animal abuse, 35, 40
Antidepressant medications, 43
Anxiety, 18, 44
Apologies, 107
Arguments, coping with, 106–9. *See also* Confrontation
Assertiveness training, 56
Authority, defiance of, 80–82

B

Behavioral therapy, 42
Big Book, 72, 78, 81, 98, 118
Bill W., 73
Blame, 19–20, 90–91
  common conceits and, 73
  in expressions of anger, 96
  resentments and, 66–67, 76, 78
  victim blaming, 32–33, 46
Bob, Dr., 73
Brick, the (anger style), 26–28, 81

Bulldozer, the (anger style),
25–26, 77, 81

C

Calming others, 107–9
Catastrophizing, 68–69, 108–9
Child abuse, 4, 15, 31, 35, 37–38, 55
getting help with, 40–41, 45
Chronic illness, 53–54
Codependency. *See* Nice People
(NPs) (anger style)
Cognitive therapy
for violent behavior, 42
for working through
resentments, 65
Common conceits, 72–73, 80
Confrontation, 87–88, 90, 103–12
appropriate reasons for,
98–102, 115–16, 119
arguments/fights, 106–9
limits of usefulness of, 110–12
skills for handling, 103–6
Control, of temper, 38–39
Cravings, and physiological
response to anger, 89

D

Defiance, 80–82
Denial
of addiction-related problems,
18–20, 80–82
common conceits and, 73
of emotions, 4–5, 8, 49, 92
Depression
addiction and, 18
anger and, 21, 28, 34, 54
treatment for, 44
Domestic violence, 31–47. *See also*
Child abuse
control and, 38–39

gender factors, 33, 34, 37
getting help with, 39–47
help for victims, 46–47
problem described, 31–32,
33–34, 37–38
spouse abuse, 4, 15, 31, 36–37, 38
stress and, 35–37
substance abuse and, 34–35
victim blaming with, 32–33, 46
Dr. Bob, 73

E

Eating disorders, 21, 29, 53, 56
Expression of anger. *See also*
Anger styles; Confrontation
acknowledging vs., 92
definition of, 92
feeling vs., 34
inappropriate ventilation,
85–87, 88–89, 92, 106
skills for, 87, 88–89, 96
Extramarital affairs, 54

F

Family. *See also* Domestic
violence
adult children of alcoholics,
20, 50, 57–58
anger problems summarized,
6–8, 15–21
Fear, anger as expression of, 95
Fights (arguments), coping with,
106–9. *See also* Confrontation
Forgetting, and forgiveness,
118–23
Forgiveness, 8, 113–24
forgetting and, 118–23
of self, 123–24
of sins of commission, 118–23,
124

of sins of omission, 117–18, 124
trust and, 118–22
Fourth Step, 73
Freudian psychoanalysis, 42

H

Health problems, anger-related,
53–54, 87, 88
Homicidal thoughts, 5, 12
Honesty
in addictive families, 20
with therapists, 44, 56
Human Aggression (Storr), 50
Humor, as response to anger in
others, 108

I

Illness, anger-related, 53–54, 87, 88
Inventory taking, 73
I statements, 29, 96

J

James, William, 91
Jenco, Lawrence Martin, 123

L

Lightheart, the (anger style),
29–30, 81
Listening, as calming technique,
109

M

Medication
abuse of, and Nice People
anger style, 51, 57
therapy for anger problems
and, 42–43, 44–45
Money management, 53
Moral inventory, 73
Murder, thoughts of, 5, 12

N

Narcotics Anonymous (NA), 41,
57
National Association for Children
of Alcoholics (NACA), 57
Natural consequences, 63
Nice People (NPs) (anger style),
48–58
coping with, in loved ones,
57–58
getting help with, 55–57

O

Obesity, 53, 56
Overeaters Anonymous, 56
Overeating, 53, 56

P

Promiscuity, 54
Prozac, 43
Psychiatric therapy, 42, 44–45
Psychoanalysis, 42

R

Rational-emotive therapy, 42, 65
Reassurance, as calming
technique, 108–9
Recovery, 1–10, 15, 37
Relapse
accepting responsibility and, 78
uncontrolled expression of
anger and, 15
Resentments, 13, 16–17, 59–71
blame and, 66–67, 76, 78
defined, 59
listing, 64–65
with Nice People anger style,
49
questionnaire on, 70–71
sources of, 75–76

strategies for coping with, 64,
65, 68–70, 77–80, 82–84
unreasonable beliefs and,
63–66, 70–71, 90–91
Responsibility, accepting, 78

S

Self-esteem
addictive families and, 20
Nice People anger style and,
49, 50, 52, 56
Self-fulfilling prophecy, 91
Self-pity, 66–68
Self-talk, 65, 66, 68–69, 70, 78–80
during confrontations, 105
Serenity, 13, 14–15, 87, 89
Serenity Prayer, 14, 75
Sexual problems, 54
Silent treatment, 21, 107
Sleeping pills, 42–43
Smith, Robert Holbrook, 73
Sobriety, 8
Soulful One, the (anger style),
28–29, 77, 81
Spouse abuse, 4, 15, 31, 36–37, 38
help for victims, 46–47
Storr, Anthony, 50, 52
Stress
arguments and, 107
violent behavior and, 35–37
Styles, anger. *See* Anger styles
Suicide
attempts and threats, 21, 54–55
Nice People anger style and,
51, 54–55

thoughts about, 5, 12, 51

T

Therapy, 65, 88–89
for codependents, 56
for violent behavior, 42–47
Tranquilizers, 42–43
Trust, and forgiveness, 118–22

V

Ventilation, 85–87, 88–89, 92, 106.
See also Expression of anger
Victim blaming, 32–33, 46
Violent behavior, 4, 31–47. *See
also* Child abuse; Domestic violence; Suicide
as anger style, 31–39
animal abuse, 35, 40
getting help with, 39–47
with Nice People anger style,
55
spouse abuse, 4, 15, 31, 36–37,
38

W

W., Bill, 73
Wants, 74–76, 91, 94
Weapons, 40
Wilson, William Griffith, 73

Z

Zoloft, 43

About the Authors

Gayle Rosellini has worked and published widely in the field of chemical dependency. *Mark Worden* has written many articles on dependency and recovery.

HAZELDEN PUBLISHING AND EDUCATION is a division of the Hazelden Foundation, a not-for-profit organization. Since 1949, Hazelden has been a leader in promoting the dignity and treatment of people afflicted with the disease of chemical dependency.

The mission of the foundation is to improve the quality of life for individuals, families, and communities by providing a national continuum of information, education, and recovery services that are widely accessible; to advance the field through research and training; and to improve our quality and effectiveness through continuous improvement and innovation.

Stemming from that, the mission of the publishing division is to provide quality information and support to people wherever they may be in their personal journey—from education and early intervention, through treatment and recovery, to personal and spiritual growth.

Although our treatment programs do not necessarily use everything Hazelden publishes, our bibliotherapeutic materials support our mission and the Twelve Step philosophy upon which it is based. We encourage your comments and feedback.

The headquarters of the Hazelden Foundation are in Center City, Minnesota. Additional treatment facilities are located in Chicago, Illinois; New York, New York; Plymouth, Minnesota; St. Paul, Minnesota; and West Palm Beach, Florida. At these sites, we provide a continuum of care for men and women of all ages. Our Plymouth facility is designed specifically for youth and families.

For more information on Hazelden, please call **1-800-257-7800**. Or you may access our World Wide Web site on the Internet at **http://www.Hazelden.org**.

5784